EMOTIONAL INTELLIGENCE

INTELLIGENCE

FOR FUNERAL DIRECTORS

Melanie Carr, Ph.D.

EMOTIONAL INTELLIGENCE

FOR FUNERAL DIRECTORS

The Secret to Less Stress and Burnout at Work

gatekeeper press

Columbus, Ohio

Emotional Intelligence for Funeral Directors: The Secret to Less Stress and Burnout at Work

Published by Gatekeeper Press
2167 Stringtown Rd, Suite 109
Columbus, OH 43123-2989
www.GatekeeperPress.com

Library of Congress Control Number: 2020938216

ISBN (paperback): 9781662901096
eISBN: 9781662901102

This book is dedicated to my husband, Hancl Carr, for his steadfast love and belief in my abilities. I could not have done this without his support and encouragement.

Table of Contents

Foreword

I have been in the funeral profession for my entire life. In fact, after a few days of life, I moved from the hospital to the funeral home – our house was connected to the funeral home. My father was a funeral director and funeral home owner for 57 years before his death in 2005. I worked at the funeral home through high school, and upon graduating from Baylor University, I immediately went to work for Funeral Directors Life Insurance Company, where I have been for the past 35 years! So, needless to say, I am well-acquainted with stress and burnout that comes from being a funeral director.

I am extremely happy that someone has finally made an effort to address the issue of stress and burnout in the funeral profession – thank you, Melanie.

The funeral profession is tough on the people that choose to work in it. Funeral directors have to deal with long hours, a range of emotions, and difficult customer/family situations. In fact, I considered being a funeral director, however, as a junior in high school, I assisted my dad with a friend of mine who was killed in a car accident. It was more than I could handle. That's when I decided to not be a funeral director – I became an accountant, in part, to get away from the emotional impact that the funeral profession has on people in the business.

Even though I have worked in the funeral profession, at Funeral Directors Life, I have not been on the front line. I have witnessed the emotional toll this profession takes on funeral directors. I was not surprised by Melanie's findings. Through her research and data, she has proven what most of us old-timers in the profession have always thought to be the case but did not know.

Before reading Melanie's book, I knew very little about emotional intelligence (EI), and I had no knowledge of how EI impacted the funeral profession. It was interesting to find out that there is an inverse link between EI and occupational stress – the higher a person's EI, the lower their stress. The most poignant statement that Melanie made in her book was, "... no matter what your EI is today, it can always be enhanced (improved upon)!" Through education and training, people in the funeral profession can improve their EI which will help them lead less stressful lives. Very cool!

I have worked with Melanie for nine years at Funeral Directors Life, and I'm proud to say that she practices what she preaches. Her commitment to this profession and her care for the people in it is authentic. This book is proof!

As she states in the book, "It is sad that most people just do not realize the valuable role funeral directors provide in society. Funeral directors are America's *last* responders. They tend to work in the background of society, without public notice or acclaim." **Emotional Intelligence For Funeral Directors: *The secret to less stress and burnout at work*** finally sheds some light on a subject that has been ignored far too long.

I hope this book provides insight to people in the funeral profession and a direction for future education and training to help them.

Blessings,
Kris Seale
President & CEO of Funeral Directors Life Insurance Company

Prologue

As this book is being prepared to go to print in 2020, our world is battling a pandemic, COVID-19. I would be remiss if I did not speak about this virus in the context of this body of work. Everyone's lives and how we conduct business has changed. No one could have prepared for this, as this is the subject of movies, not real life. We are experiencing an unprecedented time. The world as we knew it is gone, at least for now.

Face-to-face interactions and contacts have been replaced with virtual meetings and social distancing. Hugs have been replaced with FaceTime waves. Most of the country is currently under stay-in-place orders unless individuals need to do essential business such as going to the doctor, shopping for groceries, or picking up food or medicine. Any social gathering has to be less than ten people and in some parts of the country, even that is not being allowed.

At the time of writing, only essential businesses remain open. This includes hospitals, health-care industries, police and fire departments, grocery and drugstores, some construction companies, and funeral homes. Workers in these industries are willingly exposing themselves to high risk, to help all of us.

All of these facts mean one thing ... more stress! The coronavirus did not replace all of our previous stressors.

It only added to them. Thus, people are experiencing a compound effect. If they were having marital or financial problems before the virus, now they still have to deal with those problems in addition to worries about their health and their extended family's health. People have to figure out how to help their kids at home with schoolwork. They may have lost their job and are running out of money. Times are tough and everyone is feeling it.

This book is specifically geared for funeral directors—and they are definitely feeling the weight of the current crisis. Funeral directors are considered essential employees who cannot stay at home and practice social distancing. They still have families to see, deceased bodies to embalm or cremate, and funerals to plan and orchestrate. They are playing a critical role in our society, and we especially see this in New York and New Orleans, where both areas are experiencing high numbers of COVID-19 deaths. Mortuaries and medical examiner offices are full in some areas, and more cities are likely to experience this before this crisis is over.

I hope my book can help in some small way. While we cannot avoid stress, especially during times of crisis, we can lower our stress levels by gaining control of what we can and practicing healthy, adaptive coping mechanisms and practicing good stress management techniques. My book explores another way you can lower your stress ... improving your emotional intelligence. I hope you find my research and tips valuable and helpful.

Introduction

Have you ever wondered why some people get so overwhelmed in stressful situations, while others seem calm as can be? I know I have. I have worked in several different industries and one thing I learned is you can tell a lot about people's character when they are put to the test. Some overcome and some have a meltdown.

I spent a decade working in television news and let me tell you, that is a stressful field. The goal with any news station is to find the most relevant, important news stories, and be the first to report on them. With television news, you face constant deadlines. Add any type of crisis, and the daily stress instantly escalates. I covered big news stories such as the terrorist attacks on 9/11, Hurricane Brett, and the abduction and death of a Walmart cashier in Tyler, Texas, among others.

I remember one day while I was working as a news reporter, and it was getting near the end of my shift. I felt terrible! While I did not know it at the time, I was coming down with the flu. I was praying for the night to end so I could go home, get some medicine, and crash for the night. Then all of a sudden, we had breaking news. There was a shooting in a nearby community, and my producer needed a team to head that direction immediately—so they sent my photographer and me out to the scene.

The location was a good hour away from the news station and this was right in the middle of winter, so it was freezing. We rushed to the scene and then scrambled to find the police chief to get details of what had happened so that we could go live. The stress was intense. Sick, cold, and feeling overwhelmed. Not only did I have to get the information, but I had to get it before my competitors did. We got the interview and then my photographer started setting up the live shot. Facing this time crunch along with some technical difficulties, I remember my photographer cursing and throwing things. It was not personal. He was not mad at the producer or at me. It was situational. He was stressed and this was how he reacted.

This scenario was nothing new for me. Working in television news, there was always another show coming up. We had deadlines for the 5:00 a.m., noon, 5:00 p.m., 6:00 p.m., and 10:00 p.m. newscasts. This meant tracking down interviews, writing a script, getting it approved by a producer, voicing our script, and then giving it to our photographers so they could edit their video on top of our audio. Some people handled this pressure better than others. Yelling, cursing, and throwing things were pretty standard in the back to vent frustrations. Others cried and seemed to be emotionally falling apart. A few people, though, remained calm, confident, and in control. Those were the ones we looked to for guidance, leadership, and instruction.

So, why did some lose their cool? If you asked those who remained calm, they would say the other people were simply not cut out for that kind of work. Often, that was proved correct. Individuals who got stressed out easily did not stay in the profession for long; they burned out and often quit within the first three years. We had a running bet to see who would make it that long.

That experience stayed with me as I moved into a new career working in the funeral industry. Just as before, I noticed some people could handle the emotional stress of working in the profession, while others seemed to become overwhelmed, exhausted, quickly nearing burnout. This time though, instead of just accepting that those who burned out were not cut out to be funeral directors, I decided I wanted to figure out why.

By then, I had returned to school to obtain a PhD in psychology. When it came time to decide the subject to explore for my dissertation, I immediately knew that I wanted to look at occupational stress. I began my research and learned so much through the process. I hope my discovery helps you lower your stress and your risk for burnout.

All Stressed Out

It does not matter what industry you research. Occupational stress is very common and occurs in any workplace. There can be many different factors that contribute to stressing a person out, but one thing is clear ... all that stress can adversely affect a person.

Not only is work stress a universal problem, but in my research I found that it is also the leading form of stress for adults[1]. A founding researcher on stress, Hans Selye, believed that stress is simply a response to anything that sets off an alarm in a person. If a person perceives that stress to be harmful or bad, a strain can be felt almost immediately[2]. What is most concerning about work stress is the fact that it appears to be on the rise. One study found that 36% of Americans stated their job is causing them major stress[3], and another found that reports of work stress have risen 18% in the last five years[4].

These statistics should not be surprising. It seems like more demands are being placed on employees all the time. The more you can do, the more that is expected of you, right? I've heard people say, "You just can't feed the beast enough," and I get it. Year after year, employers expect better results. That means it is up to employees to perform up to these ever-escalating standards, and that's where the problem comes in.

What Causes Occupational Stress

In the simplest terms, if your job demands exceed your ability, either actual or perceived, you will start to feel occupational stress. According to the Job Demands-Resources (JDR) model[5], strain occurs when there is an imbalance between required job tasks and the physical, psychological, organizational, or social factors that help people achieve their goals. If you feel like you can do a task, you can do it relatively effortlessly, but if those demands outweigh your resources or ability, you end up feeling overwhelmed.

Work demands can have a cumulative effect on a person as well. While you can handle some demands, as those demands increase, so will your occupational stress level. These work demands come in two forms: quantitative and qualitative. Quantitative demands include such things as work hours and physical duties, while qualitative demands include emotional duties such as consoling a grieving family member[6].

The conservation of resources (COR) theory tries to explain why people experience occupational stress. According to COR theory, people try to build up and enhance their resources to prepare for any demands that come their way[7]. Resources can be anything from personal possessions, money, and time, to personal characteristics like perseverance or drive. It is like those video games where people go into combat and try to win different weapons in preparation for any scenario. The same mentality applies to work. We stockpile resources so that we will be ready to handle any challenge. But we cannot be prepared for everything at all times. When demands outweigh our resources, we experience a resource loss, which then triggers feelings of stress.

We use up our resources not only at work, but also when we handle personal and family issues, or when dealing with people during our free time. If we experience high demands in one area of our life, we have fewer resources available to use in other areas. So, while you may generally be able to handle all of your work duties, if you go through a death in your own family or are going through a divorce or other personal issues, you may find yourself unable to simultaneously handle work demands. That is because you are experiencing what is known as a loss spiral[8].

Burnout

According to Hans Selye[9], people go through three stages when exposed to stress:

1. Alarm
2. Resistance
3. Exhaustion.

When a person faces a stressor, it triggers an alarm, which, if possible, will result in that person changing the situation to avoid that stress. Some work demands can trigger acute stress that occurs suddenly after a person faces a new task or problem. If stress continues and is considered chronic, a person will find a way to compensate. But, if the stressor continues for an excessive length of time or is constant, it will trigger physical and emotional exhaustion.

Constant exposure to stress at work is a significant contributor to job burnout. People can often handle moments of stress, but when that stress does not go away, it starts to eat away at a person. Constant stress also erodes people's hope. When a person cannot see a better future or set any goals and starts to develop feelings of hopelessness, Viktor Frankl states that people start to experience what he terms a provisional existence[10]. It is at this stage that numerous kinds of diseases can develop. Chronic stress can have adverse long-term negative effects on a person's well-being.

Would you believe that close to one in three people experience burnout[11]? That sounds exceptionally high. But when you look at the components that make up burnout, you may be able to see signs in yourself or one of your coworkers.

Burnout has three components—emotional exhaustion, depersonalization, and a lack of feeling personal accomplishment[12]. Emotional exhaustion is the most common symptom and is a feeling of being overextended or emotionally spent. Depersonalization occurs when a person feels detached from themselves or has a callous attitude. A person at this stage may act in an uncaring manner or seem very unsympathetic to what others are going through. Both depersonalization and cynicism are coping mechanisms that help people to distance themselves from a stressor psychologically[13]. Finally, a lack of personal accomplishment is the feeling of not being able to reach one's goals.

Causes of Burnout

So, what is causing all this burnout? While researching this topic, I found experts cite four main reasons. The first and most common is caseload size. That is probably not too surprising. If people feel like they are being overworked and have too much on their plate, it seems evident that they will start to feel exhausted and burned out.

Other factors that may contribute to feelings of burnout include organizational setting, age, sex, and educational level. A job's environment poses different challenges. In terms of work setting, the research I found was mixed. One study found that human services employees working in a rural setting experienced a higher feeling of burnout because the rural setting isolated them and limited their resources[14]. But another study involving physicians found that workers in urban settings have higher job demands, higher levels of exhaustion, and less job control[15].

Age and gender are also contributing factors, but again my research found mixed indications as to how these factors correlate with stress and burnout. One study involving older employees found that this demographic receives less managerial attention and support, which leads to feelings of emotional exhaustion[14]. Another study, though, found that physicians under the age of fifty are at increased risk of burnout[16].

There are mixed findings regarding gender, as well. One study[14] involving older employees found that males experienced more feelings of burnout than did women, and another study[17] involving medical personnel found that men were higher for both emotional exhaustion and depersonalization. However, there have been other studies indicating that women are at a higher risk. One study looking at burnout rates among surgery residents found that women were at a higher risk, possibly because of the additional demands upon them at home and the fact that they worked in a male-dominated field.[11] Another study involving physicians also found women were at higher risk, which was concerning since more women are entering this profession[16]. These two studies made me think about the funeral industry since more women are becoming funeral directors, yet many would still say this is a male-dominated profession.

Some stressful situations can still put even resilient individuals at risk for burnout. Some contend that people with high resiliency are prone to act and take control of a situation, but during a crisis that may then lead to excessive work, which can lead to burnout[18].

Effects of Stress

Stressful events at work can affect people emotionally, physically, and cognitively. Emotionally, stressors can cause feelings of tension, anxiety, and depression. Anxiety is likely the first reaction a person experiences since it tends to occur right after a person encounters a stressor[2]. One study looking at people recently diagnosed with either depression or general anxiety disorder found that 45% were experiencing workplace stress[1]. Excessive stress, or chronic stress that is ongoing and unresolved, has been linked with mental illness[19], and cognitive effects of stress may appear within a person as he/she starts to lose patience, or becomes suspicious of other people[20].

Physically, a person under constant stress may experience headaches, migraines, ulcers, and asthmatic attacks[20]. Researchers have also found a link between stress and more severe health conditions such as coronary heart disease and strokes[21]. There is also a connection between stress and cancer, with one study finding that over 50% of cancer cases were linked to work stress[22].

Occupational stress is not only a hazard for employees, but it affects employers as well. Employees experiencing stress have diminished quality, productivity, and overall well-being[23]. Annually, occupational stress accounts for over a billion dollars lost due to turnover and absenteeism[24]. Burnout ultimately affects job performance as fatigued employees are either unwilling or unable to exert more effort, which leads to them disengaging altogether or functioning at less than optimal levels[25].

Work stress has wide-reaching adverse effects, but why do some people seem more immune to it than others? Well, according to Selye[9], stress can either be deemed eustress (optimal stress) or distress (negative stress) depending on how a person interprets a stressor[26]. Eustress is a positive type of stress. It helps people develop feelings of confidence, fulfillment, and meaning, which helps them deal with stress[27], whereas distress is harmful because it causes anxiety and apathy, which can impede problem-solving[28]. Selye also contended that conditioning factors like diet, exercise, heredity, and previous stress conditioning may alter people's reactions to stress[9]. This theory helped him explain why some people become overwhelmed in stressful situations, and some are better able to cope with it.

Questions to Ponder

1. How would you rate your current stress level at work on a scale from 1-10, with a 1 indicating very low stress and a 10 indicating high stress?

_____

_____

_____

2. What causes you the most stress at work?

_____

_____

_____

3. How is stress affecting you physically or mentally?

_____

_____

_____

4. Is your work stress affecting your personal life? If so, how?

_____

_____

_____

5. What are you doing to help yourself de-stress?

_____

_____

_____

CHAPTER 2 The Challenges Facing Funeral Directors

I have been working in the funeral industry for the past decade. My career has been as a business and marketing advisor, market center manager, and pre-need sales representative in Texas. I have worked with funeral homes from the valley to the state's capital and now in the Dallas/ Fort Worth area. Working with various funeral homes and funeral directors has given me a unique perspective on the problem of occupational stress.

Whenever I tell people I work in the funeral industry, I hear the same responses. "Why?" "Isn't that awfully depressing?" "I could never do that." This is because often people think if you work in the funeral industry, you must be dealing with dead bodies, and most people I come across are simply uncomfortable with death. They cannot imagine working with a family that just lost their loved one. That emotional stress would be too much. I'm sure that funeral directors have heard these same sentiments from many other people. It takes a unique person to be able to handle the different components required to be a funeral director.

At a funeral convention, I once heard that 50% of funeral directors leave the profession in the first five years. Yikes! That is an incredibly high turnover rate and indicates the industry needs to do something to stop funeral directors from burning out.

Stigma versus Reality

Being a funeral director is hard work and full of stigmas. Funeral directors are frequently portrayed negatively by the media[29]. Society often perceives funeral directors as people who benefit from death or another person's tragedy[30]. Plus, society habitually stigmatizes funeral directors as doing "dirty work" since funeral directors deal with dead bodies and this is perceived as a physical taint[31].

These stigmas are largely unspoken, but they are very real. If you want to stop any conversation, simply tell people you work in the funeral industry. You will get looks of revulsion, wonder, and even judgment. A friend of mine describes this as the "yuck" factor. Most people cannot imagine working around dead bodies and that makes them question why you would. One funeral director I know feels this is because our society does not want to talk or think about death. It's almost like a taboo subject. People seem to think that as long as they don't talk about death, it won't happen to their family.

It is sad that most people just do not realize the valuable role funeral directors provide in society. Funeral directors are America's last responders. They tend to work in the background of society, without public notice or acclaim[32]. People are not cheering for them or putting signs of support up on their front lawns.

Yet, funeral directors play a critical role in our society. Their handling of the deceased is vital to public health[32]. They work rain or shine during both normal and crisis situations.

Funeral directors experienced a challenging situation when the AIDS crisis first began. Similarly, funeral directors in 2020 feel anxious about the coronavirus and their exposure to it but are resolved to do their job[33]. That means they have to come to work and handle the bodies of both confirmed and suspected coronavirus deaths, albeit with fewer staff members and more safety measures in place.

Most people probably do not realize that the funeral industry even has disaster teams. These state and national disaster teams respond to mass casualty situations. Remember Hurricane Katrina back in 2005? Over fourteen hundred people died as a result of that catastrophe[33]. While local funeral directors in Louisiana helped, they were quickly overwhelmed and needed help from disaster teams.

Stigmas and some of these real threats are just a few of the stressors that may help explain the high turnover rate in this industry. I already mentioned the statistic that 50% of funeral directors leave the industry within the first five years[34], but another statistic says the problem is much worse. An industry insider claims that statistic rises to 70% when one looks at the first ten years funeral directors work in this field[35]. Wow! That number is shocking and is much higher than I would have expected.

Job Demands

Some of the stress funeral directors experience is a result of the job's demanding duties. Funeral directors become involved in a case following a person's death when they are called to the scene to collect and transport the body into their care. This pick-up can be at the scene of a car accident, in a hospice facility, or on the third floor of a walk-up. These pick-ups expose funeral directors to what is known as critical incident stress. Critical incident stress is a stress that lasts two days to four weeks after a person has witnessed or experienced a tragedy, death, or near-death threatening situation[36]. As a result of that exposure, a person may experience chest pains, high blood pressure, or unwanted mental images[37]. If not managed, critical incident stress can lead to posttraumatic stress and burnout[38].

The funeral director profession has many challenging physical aspects such as lifting a body onto a stretcher. Moving and lifting bodies puts funeral directors at higher risk for low back pain and musculoskeletal problems[39]. They also have some physical tasks that can be deemed gruesome, depending on the cause of death. They may have to tie down extremities, clean the body, and remove any drains, tubes, or lines put in place while the deceased was in the hospital. Funeral directors also have to stitch up any lacerations and may need to wire the jaws shut while pressing out any sunken cheeks to restore a lifelike appearance.

Visually those tasks can be quite daunting, but it is the smell that funeral directors say they struggle with the most[40]. The smell of death and decomposition is not something easily forgotten. Even after significant time has passed, a similar smell can trigger disturbing memories. To carry out these functions, funeral directors need some form of emotional detachment or routinizing of the work to help them focus on the task at hand, instead of focusing on what they are doing or whom they are embalming[41].

Another challenging physical aspect of the job is the long hours. Many funeral directors are required to do body pick-ups at all hours, sometimes on minimal sleep.

Sleep deprivation causes fatigue and additional stress[42], and researchers have linked it to many health issues. One study found that working more than fifty-five hours a week gives a person a one to three times greater risk for a stroke and a slightly higher risk for coronary heart disease[21].

Funeral directors also carry out tasks that carry with them some potential health hazards. Preparing the deceased for viewing exposes funeral directors to formaldehyde, a common ingredient used in embalming fluids. Formaldehyde has been linked with higher amyotrophic lateral sclerosis (ALS) mortality rates[43] and has been classified as a hazardous substance for humans[44].

People Problems

Without question, the job of funeral directing is unique. Not only are funeral directors dealing with dead bodies and grieving family members daily, but their relationship with a bereaved family poses many unique challenges. One challenge is that no one wants to be at a funeral home or use the services, which can lead to tense and even hostile interactions. The fact that no one wants this service is known as negative demand, and this makes funeral services one of the most distasteful of all consumer services[45].

Research indicates that people working in health-care professions experience a disproportionately higher amount of burnout since their jobs require more interactions with other people[46]. The same is valid for funeral directors, which explains why they are at risk for moderate to high levels of burnout[14]. One funeral director I spoke with said, "This job can consume you," and warned that if you are not careful, "you give so much to it that you have nothing left."

Caring for the deceased and their families is hugely personal, emotional, and physical. One funeral director described his job as "like a lobster inside of that pot where you slowly increase the heat." To say their job is stressful seems like an understatement.

Funeral directors handle an estimated 2.6 million deaths a year[47], and according to industry experts, those numbers are expected to steadily increase over the next thirty years as the baby boomer generation ages[33]. That means funeral directors are touching millions of lives annually when you take into account not only the deceased but the deceased's family members and friends.

A term frequently heard in the care industries is compassion fatigue, which, although similar, is different from burnout. Compassion fatigue is a type of secondary traumatic stress. It is unique to helping professions because it results from exposure to another person's suffering and results in a loss of compassionate energy for others[48]. One funeral director I spoke to said that while she understood that a person is upset because they lost a loved one, she still "just doesn't get all their emotions." Compassion fatigue includes both exhaustion and feeling more negative feelings.

Another challenge for funeral directors is dealing with time demands. Most people coming to the funeral home to make arrangements following a family member's death are facing time demands and often do not know what they are supposed to do in these situations. All this while they are emotionally grieving their loss. Most of these interactions with the deceased's family are brief, usually only lasting a couple of days. There has likely been no previous relationship between the parties, nor will there be one after the funeral, adding further challenges[30]. Funeral directors also must be proficient at many different roles occurring at the same time; counselor, manager, and salesman. The time frame to carry out all job duties is also unique. When you consider that both a wedding and a funeral have some of the same elements—flowers, booking a facility, a reception dinner with food and drinks, select clothing, and decorations—you can start to understand one aspect of why a funeral director's job is so challenging. Planning a wedding usually takes months or even a year. Now imagine doing that in two days. That is what funeral directors must do routinely.

This time restriction adds another vital aspect to consider when looking at occupational stressors. Since a funeral is often the final farewell, there are extreme risks to the funeral home if there are mistakes. Those mistakes can be devastating to family members[49]. Funeral directors feel it is their job to create a "perfect" or flawless funeral, which puts a great deal of pressure on them.

A funeral director told me this was the most challenging aspect of the job for them. They described the quest for perfection as part of the unforgiving aspect of this industry. They said they know that if "anything goes wrong, it affects the family for the rest of their life."

Emotional Labor

Another stressor that funeral directors face relates to the consequences of emotional labor. Emotional labor is work that requires people to suppress their true feelings in order to display appropriate job-related emotions. The display rules for funeral directors include suppressing feelings of irritation, keeping a neutral expression, and showing sympathy, all while handling very emotional situations. But hiding negative emotions, like anger and irritation, is often linked to higher instances of exhaustion, a symptom of burnout[50].

These rules are mandatory because a funeral director needs to communicate, empathize, and comfort clients[51]. According to traditional display rules for most organizations, people need to hide negative emotions and show positive ones. One funeral director I spoke with said it just would not be professional to be seen crying at the funeral home. This was a common sentiment that most shared with me. Another one said, "You would just like to boohoo with them, but you can't."

Many funeral directors may feel sadness and empathy when working with families. However, the unspoken display rules of the funeral industry often require them to suppress those emotions. The funeral director needs to appear to be solemn and in control, regardless of how a family is acting or what emotions they are displaying[52]. Some recommend that funeral directors should always adhere to a compassionately detached strategy with clients, in which they keep an emotional distance from death so that they can do their jobs effectively[40].

Emotional labor, although necessary, has some potentially harmful side effects associated with burnout, which include emotional exhaustion, depersonalization, and feelings of diminished accomplishments. One reason is that displaying fake emotions requires more significant effort, which leads to fatigue. It leads to feelings of being inauthentic and this emotive dissonance or conflict between inner emotions and those expressed can cause psychological distress[53].

Funeral directors handle many emotional demands and must adhere to the industry's display rules, but they may become accustomed to feeling one way and acting another. If they do, then this emotional labor may not negatively affect their stress levels. Some argue that emotional work affects all employees' well-being[51], so clearly, more research is needed.

Questions to Ponder

1. What are the most challenging tasks with your job?

   _____

   _____

   _____

2. What do you wish the public better understood about the funeral industry?

   _____

   _____

   _____

3. Do you feel like you must adhere to emotional display rules? Explain how.

   _____

   _____

   _____

4. How has compassion fatigue affected you or your coworkers?

   _____

   _____

   _____

Our Emotions at Play

Our Brain and Emotions

First, let's talk about how our brain processes emotions. It should be noted that cognitive-emotional interactions are a somewhat controversial subject[13]. While much is known about how emotions are triggered and processed, research is constantly being done to prove beliefs and assumptions.

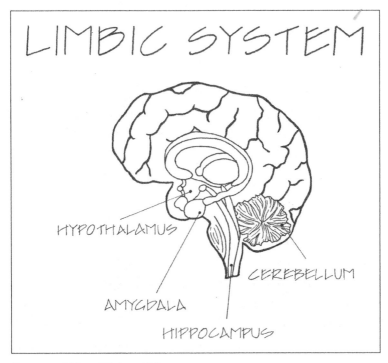

Courtesy: Kelsey Kliebert Toler

From my research, here is what I have learned. Both our nervous system and brain contribute to our feelings, but our limbic system is particularly integral to our behavioral and emotional responses. When exposed to stress, our body responds with behavioral changes and visceral responses, both of which are often automatic[54]. Imagine you are outside walking your dog, and when you turn the corner, you come upon a curled up, hissing snake. You may notice your heart rate increases, or you start excessively sweating, or you may even just freeze place.

This stressor triggers the limbic system in our brain, which includes the hypothalamus, the thalamus, the hippocampus, and the amygdala. The role of the limbic system is to help us feel and react. While each structure is involved with emotion, I want to highlight those that play key roles.

First, let's talk about the amygdala. The amygdala is our primitive emotional control structure. The amygdala is behind the fight or flight reaction to stressors when instead of thinking, we react. The amygdala controls our fear circuit. It is in charge of processing our fear and then deciding on the best course of action. Returning to the snake example, in that situation, you may react by running away or grabbing a stick to defend yourself.

The hippocampus plays a significant supporting role when it comes to emotions. It helps to put the emotional situation into context[54]. It is the hippocampus that takes our emotional experiences and helps create memories[55]. Our recall of events and our self-knowledge plays a significant role in how we then access or evaluate other similar situations. For example, if someone yelled at you frequently when you were a child, you can learn to fear situations where someone else appears unhappy or displeased with you. A related area in the brain is our prefrontal cortex. While not technically a part of our limbic system, it still plays an important role in our emotional life. The prefrontal cortex is the covering on the front of our frontal lobe. It helps with higher- functioning thoughts like determining right from wrong and choosing the best action to take. In that respect, the prefrontal cortex helps us with goal-oriented behavior[56]. The prefrontal cortex also helps regulate emotions and other emotional processes[57].

Fear can be triggered by different information processing pathways[58]. If someone does not have good insight into their reactions, the information is transmitted to the amygdala through a lower-order pathway. Such people tend to be more reactionary. When people do have good insight into their emotional reactions, the information is transmitted via a higher-order pathway. This suggests that these people will react more slowly by assessing the situation first.

The good news is that we can strengthen our prefrontal cortex through interactions with people. As this area of our brain develops, we become more likely to rationalize stressful situations and less likely to just be reactionary. This means that we can develop mental resiliency, which helps us to see stressors as challenges and not insurmountable problems.

Emotional Intelligence

So, what exactly is emotional intelligence (EI)? When I mention EI, I sometimes get an eye roll, often accompanied by a condescending head nod. People sometimes either think that EI is not necessary, or they have a misconception that EI is some touchy-feely kind of psychology. In actuality, EI relates to a person's ability to process and use emotional information to advance relationships.

EI is not the same as a person's IQ or intelligence quota. IQ is our intellectual aptitude or capability to evaluate and solve problems[59]. IQ tests assess both verbal and nonverbal problem-solving abilities by asking questions relating to pattern-driven problems, analogies, classifications, and our ability to use visual, spatial, or logical clues to determine the correct answer. Testers compare a person's score on an IQ test to others of the same age. Scores follow a bell-shaped curve, with most people falling in the middle of the curve with a score of 85 to 115, and fewer people exhibiting either extremely high or low scores[60].

When first developed, experts used IQ tests to see if children had learning disabilities. Over time though, IQ tests have become the standard method for measuring a child's cognitive abilities and predicting success in school[60]. Studies have shown that our IQ is stable by the time we are ten years old[60]. If you took the same IQ test you did as a child, your score would show little fluctuation. That means something else has to be at play when it comes to our successes in our work life as adults.

EI, on the other hand, is our ability to manage behavior and make decisions to achieve our goals, all while dealing with social nuances. Some argue that EI is more important than a person's IQ because, at its core, EI is about how you relate with others to get things done[61]. I think we have all known people who are very book smart, yet they seem socially awkward or lack common sense. What they actually lack is emotional intelligence.

As I started to think about EI, I wondered whether different psychological competencies, such as EI, could help explain why some people burn out or develop a stress-related illness and other people thrive. To gain a better understanding of EI, we should start by looking at the theoretical underpinnings and research on the topic.

According to Mayer and Salovey[62], pioneers of EI research, EI is made up of four components: perceiving, understanding, managing, and utilizing emotions. Simply put, perceiving emotions is how one recognizes emotions from nonverbal cues. Understanding emotion is the ability to know what might be causing a person's feelings. Managing emotions is the ability to regulate our emotions. Finally, utilizing emotion is how we use our knowledge about emotions and behaviors to obtain a desired goal.

EI is said to help people feel more in control, confident, and rational[63]. Self-awareness is critical with EI. One has to understand one's own emotions and be able to regulate them to achieve goals. EI is also related to having excellent interpersonal skills and adaptability, essential skills necessary to maintain a positive mood and increase stress tolerance[1].

Many experts consider EI to be an ability. As such, training can help a person improve EI skills[64], unlike our IQ, which is set by the age of ten. Training exercises not only increase EI scores but also increase a person's resilience, which helps him/her deal with stressful situations at work[65].

How EI Helps

EI has many benefits for people and organizations. People with high levels of EI are said to be better able to handle adverse life events[66] in terms of how they manage their emotions. People with high EI make great employees because they are more outcome-focused[67]. That means they keep their eyes on the end goal and aren't focused on obstacles that crop up along the way. People with high EI are better able to analytically review the context of a situation before deciding how to react[68]. This is their risk assessment ability. They can analyze the situation and respond intellectually, instead of just being reactionary. Finally, people with high EI are better at following the display rules for the situation they are in[67]. This may mean that they are better at using tact and decorum, and therefore appear more professional in their words and actions.

In the workplace, EI is a predictive element in employee outcomes. It is linked to better job performance[68], higher job satisfaction[69], and higher self-efficacy[70]. People with high EI are confident in their abilities, achieve their goals, and are overall happier employees.

People with high EI are also great team players. They are better at building cohesiveness with the people they work with by understanding, empathizing, and supporting each other's job demands and duties[71]. Also, people with high EI remain more focused on the company's goals and objectives[71], instead of just looking at what's in it for them.

Finally, those with higher EI have less emotional dissonance or conflict between felt and expressed emotions. This means they are able to appropriately express what they are feeling. Having good mood congruence is an important skill when working in emotional labor professions[72]. Emotional labor encompasses any job that requires employees only to express certain feelings while suppressing those deemed inappropriate for the clients that their business serves.

A funeral director told me it would be "inappropriate to cry" or break down because "the family needs you to be in control" and take care of them. Other funeral directors shared that sentiment. They said you never let a family see you cry. If you feel your emotions getting the better of you, then you leave the room. Several mentioned the need to wear their "mask" or "put on their poker face" when dealing with family members. Yet in these cases, it appeared there was a selfless reason why these funeral directors were not expressing their true emotions. As one funeral director put it, personal feelings cannot come into the arrangement room because then "it becomes about me, and not what the family is going through."

Mixed review of EI and Work Stress

Numerous studies over the last ten years have explored the relationship between EI and stress. What I discovered in my research was that findings on the subject are mixed. While some studies have shown positive benefits with stress as a result of higher EI, others find no relationship or even an inverse relationship.

The studies that found that the higher a person's EI, the lower their occupational stress, revealed some commonalities. These studies found that people with higher EI have lower cortisol secretion, which is a physiological reaction to stress[73], can minimize stressful feelings[74], and see stressful situations as a challenge rather than as a threat[75], which may preclude a stress response from occurring.

But despite the overwhelmingly positive evidence of EI's effects on stress, not all the findings have been in agreement. Some researchers found that people with high EI experience more stress compared to their counterparts, such as when being exposed to a new task[76] or when facing a short-term performance challenge[73]. People with high EI may also experience more distress at work because they are more in tune with mood stimuli[77]. Those with higher EI experienced higher psychological strain and feelings of job insecurity because they were overly sensitive to others' emotions, so any negative emotions related or directed towards them made them feel like their job was in jeopardy[78].

The majority of studies I analyzed showed EI as something that helps people achieve many positive outcomes and protects them from any adverse consequences. Despite these findings, EI did not help all people in all situations. During my research, I noticed that the dynamics of EI and occupational stress were not explicitly analyzed in terms of how they affect funeral directors.

After three years of research, reading countless articles, interviewing funeral directors about their experiences, and analyzing and synthesizing hundreds of pages of data, I found an inverse link between EI and occupational stress: the higher a funeral director's EI, the lower the occupational stress. This discovery is exciting news because since EI is an ability, no matter what your EI is today, it can always be enhanced!

Questions to Ponder

1. Do you tend to be quick to react, or are you someone who thinks before acting?

2. How would you rate your emotional intelligence on a scale of 1-10 (with 1 indicating low EI, and 10 indicating high EI)?

3. Of the four EI components (perceiving, understanding, managing, and utilizing emotions), which ones do you need to work on improving?

4. Are you willing to work on your EI skills, or do you think they are "good enough"?

My Research

Now that I had a good understanding of the potential of EI as a mitigating factor in minimizing stress' impact on a person, I decided I wanted to do my research looking specifically at funeral directors. I developed the following research questions that served as a guide for my study:

1. How do funeral directors experience stressful situations at work?
2. How do funeral directors deal with stressful situations at work?
3. How is EI reflected in the ways funeral directors deal with stressful situations at work?

Research Methodology and Design

For this study, I chose to use a qualitative methodology. This type of research relies primarily on interviews, observations, texts, or data obtained from focus groups or archival materials in order to learn about the meaning people ascribe to events, actions, or beliefs[79]. Qualitative studies see participants more like co-researchers helping to uncover the truth while realizing that everyone's experiences are different. Since I wanted to learn about funeral directors' lived experiences, I needed to hear from them directly on the meanings of their experiences.

Specifically, I took an interpretative phenomenological design approach to this research. Phenomenology strives to understand how people make sense of events and find meaning in their experiences. Interpretative phenomenology values the researchers' insight and analysis, believing their involvement in the research influences people's experiences[80] and therefore researchers play a key aspect in the meaning-making[81].

For this study, the phenomenon of interest was how funeral directors experience and deal with stressful situations at work. I discovered my findings through my exchanges with participants and my interpretations of their behaviors.

Participants

I knew the general population for this study needed to be licensed and employed funeral directors in the United States. While it would have been interesting to interview funeral directors that left the profession, that population would be difficult to track down. To make this study feasible, I then narrowed down my focus to consider funeral directors currently licensed and employed in Texas.

I chose to do purposive sampling because this is a technique of selecting participants based on their qualities, knowledge, or experience they possess[82]. This sampling method also adheres to the theoretical underpinnings of phenomenology, which recommends selecting people based on their relevance to the phenomenon and important predetermined variables[80]. The predetermined variables of interest for this study were the funeral directors' years of experience, gender, work setting, and age. I felt these variables were significant because each could affect a person's stress levels.

I used quota sampling to ensure my final sample had a minimum number of participants in each of the categories. Eventually, my study included eleven funeral directors. This sample size ensured that I had enough participants from each group to look for a commonality of experiences. The final breakdown included:

- Four funeral directors from urbanized areas
- Six female funeral directors
- Nine funeral directors with over five years' experience
- Three funeral directors under the age of forty.

Some of the participants fell into more than one category (see Table 1). The majority of participants were white (72.7%), between the ages of 41-55 (54.5%), and married (72.7%). Fifty percent had been licensed funeral

Table 1. Demographics of Participants

Partici-pant	Age Range	Gender	Marital Status	Years Licensed	Setting	Role
#1	41-55	M	Single	20 yrs. +	Rural	FDIC
#2	41-55	F	Married	5-10 yrs.	Rural	FDIC
#3	56+	M	Married	20 yrs. +	Urban	FD
#4	41-55	M	Married	20 yrs. +	Urban	Owner/FD
#5	41-55	M	Married	20 yrs. +	Rural	FD/Embalmer
#6	26-40	F	Married	5-10 yrs.	Rural	FDIC
#7	41-55	F	Married	15-20 yrs.	Urban	Owner/FD
#8	41-55	F	Married	10-15 yrs.	Suburb	FDIC
#9	56+	M	Divorced	20 yrs. +	Urban	FD
#10	26-40	F	Single	< 5 yrs.	Suburb	FD/Embalmer
#11	26-40	F	Married	< 5 yrs.	Suburb	FD/Embalmer

directors for over 20 years. The setting fluctuated with four working in a rural setting (36.4%), four working in an urban setting (36.4%), and three working in a suburban setting (27.3%). Roles also varied among participants. Four were funeral directors in charge (36.4%); two were funeral directors only (18.2%); two were owners and operators of funeral homes (18.2%); and three were funeral directors and embalmers (27.3%).

Sources of Data

This study incorporated interviews that I conducted one-on-one and face-to-face with those eleven funeral directors. The interviews lasted anywhere from thirty to seventy minutes. I ended the conversations only when I could obtain no new information about the phenomenon under investigation. I asked everyone the same initial questions, adjusting the questions as needed to understand each person's experiences fully.

Each session involved the use of a demographic questionnaire, the Profile of Emotional Competence (PEC) inventory, and open-ended questions from an interview guide. The demographic survey just provided primary data such as age, marital status, years employed as a funeral director, current title/role at the funeral home, funeral home location, and gender. The PEC is a self-assessed EI inventory. It asks questions about a person's perception of his/her EI skills in different situations. Finally, the interview guide was developed by reviewing studies on EI, occupational stress, and burnout. It included open-ended questions to get a better understanding of how funeral directors experience these situations and what meaning they ascribe to them based on their work in the funeral industry. The interview guide also contained questions specifically about people's experiences working as a funeral director and the unique stressors they may have experienced on the job.

Results

I used the PEC to obtain participants' self-reported EI competencies. Scores on the PEC can range from one to five. A score of one indicates a very low EI, whereas a score of five indicates a high EI. The average global score among participants was 3.83.

The PEC also breaks down a person's EI by looking at interpersonal and intrapersonal ability. Interpersonal intelligence affects our ability to work with other people in order to get things done. Some say that this type of intelligence results in the highest pay[83]. If you are able to persuade or influence other people, you are better situated to help your company achieve its desired end. The average interpersonal score from my study was 3.71.

Intrapersonal intelligence, on the other hand, relates to how well you know yourself. What are your strengths and what are your weaknesses? This type of intelligence requires a high level of introspection or thinking about your thoughts and behaviors. Those that have good introspection have better self-awareness and better self-acceptance. The average intrapersonal score in my study was 3.96. The interpersonal and intrapersonal scores indicate that the funeral directors I spoke with, as a whole, have above-average EI.

This study sought to learn how funeral directors experience and deal with stressful situations at work, as well as to discover indications of their EI by observing their actions. After completing my analysis of the data collected through the interviews, I made some crucial discoveries. Following is a summary of the study findings. Then we will explore each finding in more depth.

Key Findings

1. Perception affects the type of stress experienced
2. Women experience more stress
3. Younger workers are more prone to stress
4. Rural settings cause more challenges
5. Adaptive coping strategies can help people to deal with stress
6. Maladaptive coping strategies can cause harm
7. Higher EI is linked to lower stress

Finding #1: Perception affects the type of stress experienced

---

Not surprisingly, experiencing stressful situations at work seemed to be a common occurrence for all participants. Everyone I interviewed stated that they had experienced stress at some time or another, which resulted in some level of anxiety. As one funeral director commented, "Being a funeral director is seriously incredibly stressful."

But what I discovered from the interviews is that some circumstances triggered feelings of distress, while others triggered feelings of eustress. This led to my first finding that a person's perception of the situation determined which type of stress they would experience.

When a funeral director saw a stressful situation at work as something threatening, it triggered feelings of distress. Except for three participants, all the funeral directors described having feelings of distress at least some of the time but with varying degrees. The most commonly expressed distressful situations at work had to do with angry clients. Funeral directors described being either yelled at, threatened, or insulted.

In fact, one funeral director shared an experience that left her feeling extremely vulnerable. She told me that one family member was upset because they were not involved in the arrangements. As a result, he cussed the funeral director out and threatened to "kick her ass." The director not only called the police to be at the service, but she also made sure to conceal carry a weapon for protection.

Other funeral directors also felt distress in handling tragic cases such as infant deaths. They said those deaths are extremely hard because there is no "why" to explain them and people want answers. One person said those kinds of deaths are hard because "they cannot get their heads around it."

The funeral directors showing the most significant signs of emotional strain talked about having feelings of anxiety and being overwhelmed. One funeral director said they felt they were "stretched too thin" and were just "overloaded with work and a lack of time." Others complained about having disenfranchised grief.

Disenfranchised grief is grief that a person cannot openly mourn. Since funeral directors deal with deaths and grieving families as a part of their job, many stated that they felt like they could not talk about their sadness related to that experience with their friends or family. As one funeral director stated, "If you are not in the business, it's hard to know what it's like every day. It's hard to understand what funeral directors go through."

A couple of funeral directors also indicated they had less patience with employees or had become suspicious of other people's intentions. They appeared to have a cynical attitude toward some families' intentions or behaviors. Instead of giving bereaved individuals the benefit of the doubt in stressful situations, these funeral directors assumed the worst. For example, when one funeral director was explaining why a family member was upset and yelling, they said it was "just his personality" or regarding a different individual, they commented, "They must be bipolar." These are signs of depersonalization, which is one component of burnout and could also be a sign of compassion fatigue.

Only one of the participants seemed at the point of job burnout and complained about ongoing work stressors out of their control. Things like not enough support from the owners, feeling overextended, and not feeling appreciated were the major complaints. These problems had been ongoing for some time and while the funeral director had complained to management, nothing had been done to help improve the situation.

This progression of feelings coincides with Selye's 1950 theory on general adaptation syndrome. As discussed earlier, Selye[9] argued that when exposed to a stressor, a person will first enter the alarm phase, then the stage of resistance, and finally, the stage of exhaustion. Since this funeral director could not escape daily stressors, the person was feeling exhausted and burned out.

In some instances, though, funeral directors I spoke with saw a stressful situation at work as merely a challenge, which then triggered feelings of eustress. Instead of getting mad or upset, eight of the funeral directors were able to change their viewpoints about the situation. Examples given were situations where a client was being irrational or making impossible demands. Instead of reacting, these funeral directors provided alternative suggestions or came up with some out-of-the-box ideas.

For example, one funeral director told me about a man who came in and was just unhappy and disgruntled about everything. Instead of getting upset, this funeral director simply told the man, "I don't think we are going to be able to satisfy your needs, so here is a list of other funeral homes in the area." That got the gentleman's attention and calmed him down. He apologized for his attitude and they were able to move forward in a constructive way.

Techniques used by the participants included focusing on staying positive, putting themselves in their customers' shoes, or reflecting on how much they love their job. Meanwhile, others talked about the wisdom they had learned over the years and their ability to regulate their emotions. All but one of the funeral directors that experienced feelings of eustress described having little to no stress currently and had high job satisfaction.

Finding #2: Women experience more stress

The funeral directors exhibiting the most feelings of distress were women. They expressed feeling overwhelmed, exhausted, and burned out. One female funeral director told me that she "couldn't see herself doing this for another year." Her complaints focused on being overworked, underappreciated, and disrespected by clients, managers, and/or owners. This was a sentiment shared by other females in this study. Another participant said she'd had thoughts that she had made the wrong career choice. She stated that she was "at my wit's end."

None of the males in the study were experiencing any kind of physical symptoms or ailments. Conversely, one female funeral director was seeing a doctor for high blood pressure, and another was seeing a therapist for help dealing with feelings of anxiety and depression.

This finding coincides with other research on gender and stress. As mentioned earlier, a study examining surgery residents and burnout rates found women to be at higher risk[84]. They contended this was a result of working in a male-dominated field as well as handling additional demands at home, typically identified as care work. This includes things like housekeeping, child-rearing, and emotional labor. Emotional labor may consist of being the friend, counselor, or support system for family and friends. Women generally are most connected emotionally to other people and seek to help keep relationships positive and thriving[85].

An expert in the field of women issues pointed out that as stressful situations intensify, it is not women's professional work that suffers; it's their self-care that is impacted[86]. This could explain why some of the women in this study were experiencing some health and mental problems.

I also noticed in my study that while the male funeral directors described stressful events that had happened to them in the past, they all stated they were not feeling any stress currently, nor did they have any ongoing complaints. They seemed to be able to let events go without much thought or emotional reaction. Looking back, some could see the humor in the situation or could even admit that their actions may have intensified the situation.

One male funeral director told me how early in his career he had lost his cool with a client and almost lost the business as a result. Both parties were able to calm down after about thirty minutes and they were able to resume the at-need conference. The funeral director said that man came back to visit him about six months later and they both laughed about their heated exchange. The man also apologized for taking his anger about the situation out on the funeral director. That turned out to be a huge learning opportunity for both parties. The funeral director told me that now he realizes that he cannot take families' emotions personally. He said, "life has mellowed him out" and made him realize life is too short to get upset about little things.

Men also expressed feeling more eustress on the job. While traditionally, women are more likely to talk to people when feeling stressed[87], and men tend to align with the masculine ideals of being tough and stoic[88], adherence to gender norms did not seem to be the reason behind the higher male ratio of experiencing feelings of eustress. Overall, the men expressed much more positive comments than did their female counterpoints.

Several women made comments questioning their decision to be a funeral director or stating they would not recommend this career to anyone. The men, on the other hand, talked more about their job satisfaction and how they would not want to do anything else. Many of the males stated that being a funeral director was a calling. This spiritual component seemed to help them realize that they have a purpose or divine duty to carry out, which may be why they seemed better able to rise above small issues or stressful interactions.

***

Finding #3: Younger workers more prone to stress

I noticed a difference in stress levels based on the participants' age. The funeral directors experiencing the most negative stress effects in my study were all under the age of forty-five. The younger funeral directors also had less favorable comments about their chosen career. One commented that it has "made me a little bitter." Another said, "I wouldn't necessarily recommend it for anyone I know."

The older funeral directors seemed more relaxed and seemed to have a better understanding of the stressors because of both their job and life experiences. They were more reflective and could look at the situation from a third-party perspective to identify both parties' mistakes. As such, it seemed like the older funeral directors had learned some important lessons, which helped them better handle current situations.

Likewise, funeral directors over the age of forty-five were less reactionary in stressful situations than were their younger associates. While everyone appeared to be able to compose themselves in front of a family, the older funeral directors could leave the case at the door instead of letting it affect the rest of their day. More of the younger ones had experiences where they would break down emotionally after a stressful situation, either with anger, sadness, or both. This finding coincides with another study that found that those under the age of thirty-nine experience more negative symptoms after exposure to critical incident stress and have a higher likelihood of leaving the profession[36].

These findings coincide with previous research and assumptions about age and emotional intelligence. Researchers found that since EI is considered to be an ability, it does improve with age and experience[89]. In fact, pioneers in EI found that older participants involved in the MSCEIT, an EI ability test, did better in all four branches (perceiving, understanding, managing, and utilizing emotions)[90].

Finding #4: Rural setting causes more challenges

I looked at the funeral home setting to see if I could find any similarities in how work environment affects funeral directors' occurrences with stress. Interestingly, I noticed that those working in a rural setting seemed to be experiencing more stress than those working in urban environments. They all shared some common complaints. They faced a lack of resources, support, and were required to handle multiple job roles.

A rural setting typically equates to smaller funeral homes and fewer staff members. These so-called "rural" funeral directors were often the only funeral director on duty at times. Working solo meant they would have to help every family that walked in the door. They were responsible for organizing and conducting all elements of the funeral. These funeral directors expressed comments like "there is no break from the funeral home," "you're kind of never off," and "I always feel like I'm 'on.'"

The plethora of duties had a compound effect on them. The more that was thrown on them, the higher their stress. Not only was their workload a significant source of their complaints, but many funeral directors were resentful that they did not have help. They felt their employers did not care about them and their needs, which only seemed to intensify their reactions.

Those working in suburban and urban funeral homes did not share the same complaints. These funeral directors worked more in team environments, which provided them with emotional and physical support. Having more staff members allowed them to hand off some of their duties to their coworkers. This way they shared not only the tasks but also the responsibility of trying to keep the families happy. They also had more routine schedules with time off, so they appeared to have a better work-life balance.

> ### Finding #5: Adaptive coping strategies can help to deal with stress

When I asked the funeral directors what types of things they did to de-stress after a stressful incident, I found that all of them had some go-to coping strategies. While all the tactics seemed to work for the participants, that does not mean that these strategies are necessarily healthy or productive long-term. In fact, some strategies appeared to be possibly harmful to the participants.

Coping strategies include both adaptive and maladaptive approaches. Adaptive strategies are positive or healthy strategies. These can consist of actively trying to fix a situation, seeking advice or support, being realistic, and staying positive. Maladaptive coping strategies, on the other hand, are considered negative and unhealthy. They include disengagement, denial, self-blame, and self-distraction[91].

After experiencing feelings of distress, some funeral directors turned to de-stressors to help them cope. These de-stressors are adaptive emotional regulation (ER) strategies since they act as mediating mechanisms[92]. Some were used immediately during a stressful situation like humor or faith, while others used mental escapes and outside activities at the end of the day.

One funeral director told me his faith in God was extremely helpful, especially when going through difficult situations. Knowing that he could "go to the Lord with anything" helped to keep his stress down. Others, though, told me connecting with nature relaxed them. They said getting outside was peaceful and helped them appreciate the beauty of nature.

Seven of the participants turned to outside activities to unwind and de-stress after a tough day. The actual activities varied from golf to exercise, hunting, or restoring furniture, but all had a physical element to them. Mental escapes or distractions were almost as popular. Six participants chose activities that helped them get their minds off their work. Some of the pastimes mentioned were listening to music or watching television.

Faith seemed to play a significant role in helping some of the funeral directors, de-stress. Six participants turned to religion frequently. Some chose to pray during a crisis, while others relied on scripture to get them through. The six participants who used faith were also the participants who expressed the least amount of stress. Whether their faith changed their perspective about events, or it just helped them keep sight of the bigger picture, those participants stated that faith kept their stress levels under control.

After experiencing feelings of distress, some funeral directors turned to outside help to help them deal with stressful situations at work. Peer support is a common form of outside help that was used by the participants of this study. Getting instrumental and emotional support is an adaptive coping strategy[93]. Seven participants believed that peer support had helped them at some point in their careers. Some turned to their spouses, while others relied on friends and coworkers when they were feeling stressed out.

Finding #6: Maladaptive coping strategies can cause more harm

---

Some of the participants used maladaptive coping strategies. The three most commonly used were: (a) defense mechanisms, (b) de-stressors, and (c) outside help. After feeling distress, some funeral directors use defense mechanisms to help them cope.

Defense mechanisms are psychological strategies that help one deal with conflicts. Mature defense mechanisms include the use of humor, anticipation, rationalization, or suppression. Immature defense mechanisms include acting out, devaluation, denial, and dissociation[91].

A typical adaptive defense mechanism used in the current study was suppression. Seven participants described needing to compartmentalize or suppress any emotions they felt.

Over time, this compartmentalizing of emotions can become emotionally taxing[94]. This can become a learned behavior, so if not careful, a person can start compartmentalizing with friends and family. One funeral director told me this happened to her when at a family member's funeral service. She said she could not even grieve because she did not know how to turn off the funeral director in her.

Regarding maladaptive defense mechanisms, two were noteworthy in this study. The first involved the use of conflict avoidance. Two people described avoiding situations or conversations they suspected could become heated or controversial. One participant seemed quite aware that this was not a good practice, but the other seemed to be in denial and acted as if she were unaware of the behavior. By not addressing the situation, both individuals stated the problem grew over time.

Conflict avoidance is considered to be maladaptive. While you may avoid a discussion, you do not want to have, it does not solve any problem. You are simply sweeping the problem under the rug and it will likely rear its head again in the future.

The most common maladaptive defense mechanism noted in this study was shutting down emotionally or becoming apathetic. I noticed this apathy in four of the participants. They each made statements that indicated they either had less emotional compassion for others or they had difficulty connecting with their own emotions. They made statements about how they did not understand why a person was being so emotional or stating that even when going through something very personal and stressful, they still felt detached emotionally. One stated that they had gotten really good at "building walls and borders" with their emotions, while another said they simply don't allow themselves to "go down the rabbit hole." This reduced interest in helping others is a sign of compassion fatigue.

Finding #7: Higher EI linked to lower stress

Finally, a large part of my study consisted of determining the emotional intelligence of my participants. To determine their EI, I analyzed the participants' PEC scores and looked for instances where I could spot their EI skills in action. The goal was to find proof, based on their actions, of participants' EI skills to support their PEC scores. Specifically, I was looking for the four mental abilities identified in the Mayer and Salovey (1993) EI theory: perceiving, understanding, managing, and utilizing their own and other people's emotions.

I looked for both examples where I could recognize instances of high EI as well as patterns of behavior that indicated a low EI. I was also looking for signs of EI by analyzing a person's intrapersonal and interpersonal EI.

In looking at the participants' intrapersonal ability, I found that those with lower EI scores had challenges managing their own emotions. They complained of excessive worrying and shared stories where they were not able to control feelings of sadness or anger. Conversely, those funeral directors with higher EI scores seemed better able to leave a situation at the door or take it for its face value. They did not ruminate on a case, nor did they let it overcome their emotions.

Likewise, in terms of interpersonal skills, those with higher EI scores seemed able to determine what other people were feeling and why they were feeling that way. They exhibited the ability to control or manage those feelings and knew how to use them appropriately. Those with lower EI scores struggled with understanding and managing others' emotions. They either seemed to be out of touch emotionally to what other people were feeling or came across as being cynical or jaded.

As a result of my analysis, I determined that those funeral directors with higher EI abilities were better able to handle stressful situations at work. They could better understand and use emotions to resolve challenges. They also reported higher degrees of happiness, job satisfaction, and less stress at work.

Questions to Ponder

1. Do you tend to view stress as something positive or negative?

   _____

   _____

   _____

2. What age group and gender do you think experiences more stress and why?

   _____

   _____

   _____

3. How does your funeral home's setting (urban, rural, or suburban) affect your work stress?

   _____

   _____

   _____

4. Which finding from this study was most surprising for you and why?

   _____

   _____

   _____

Implications

This chapter focuses more on the implications of my study, both theoretical and practical. I think it is important to note that this study focused on the funeral industry, an industry that has received little scholarly attention[29]. Most of the previous studies I found that explored EI and occupational stress have looked at other helping professions such as physicians, nurses, and medical students. While funeral directing does have some commonalities with those helping professions, the challenges funeral directors face are different. The results of this study help reveal how funeral directors experience stressful situations at work and how they react to them.

Theoretical Implications

Two conceptual foundations guided the development of this research study: Mayer and Salovey's EI theory[62] and Selye's general adaptation syndrome theory[9]. This study advances both theories by looking at a new demographic; funeral directors, and their lived experiences dealing with stressful situations at work. This study supported Mayer and Salovey's theory[62] that EI is a mental ability that helps people use and understand emotions to solve problems. The study also supported the theory that people with higher EI are better at emotional regulation[67]. Except for one participant, those with high EI scores were able to manage their emotions. The one person who had difficulty managing her emotions described how she strives for perfection, so this internal desire may be the source of her excessive worrying.

Mayer and Salovey also argued that EI helps people deal with emotional situations[62]. Based on the researchers' analysis, my study's findings supported this theoretical assumption. Four of the five people with the highest EI skills exhibited during the interviews used adaptive coping strategies, healthy defense mechanisms, and frequently experienced feelings of eustress.

This study's findings support Selye's general adaptation syndrome theory[9]. One participant had reached the exhaustion or burnout level. The person was actively looking for a new job, while seven others mentioned feeling alarmed or distress, but for five of those seven, those feelings were fleeting. The other two appeared to be at the resistance stage where their stressors had become more constant, and they were trying to change their circumstances to avoid that stress.

Selye contended that people could encounter the same event, but some felt distress or eustress[9]. This study's findings support his contention. Eight of the participants had experienced situations that triggered feelings of distress, and eight also experienced situations that provoked feelings of eustress.

Finally, Selye contended that conditioning factors, things like diet, heredity, and previous stress conditioning could alter people's reactions to stress[9], thus explaining why some people are better able to cope with stress. EI was not viewed as a separate form of intelligence in the 1950s, but this study's results lend support to the notion that EI could be one of those conditioning factors.

Seven of the eleven participants I interviewed exhibited excellent EI skills by their ability to manage their emotions when experiencing a stressful situation, and six of those seven had higher than average intrapersonal EI scores. Other coping skills and experiences could have also impacted these results, so further research is needed to prove these findings.

Practical Implications

This study provides a snapshot of the experiences of eleven Texas funeral directors. Since I limited the scope of the study to only participants' lived experiences, I cannot contend that these results would be identical for all funeral directors in all parts of the county. But this research does support the theoretical assumption that EI skills help funeral directors carry out their duties and often during stressful situations.

Not all participants showed strong EI abilities in all aspects of perceiving, understanding, managing, and utilizing emotions. All of them did have strengths in at least two or more of the EI branches, and five participants showed excellent EI skills in all areas. Based on the PEC scores, all participants have an above-average EI. What my study cannot answer is whether people with a higher EI choose to enter this profession or if working in a stressful environment provides on-the-job training, which helps funeral directors enhance their EI skills.

This study did not have a baseline of the participants' EI as they entered this career field. Still, several of them talked about how they had changed emotionally since starting their careers as funeral directors. Most could provide examples of how they were better able to handle stressful situations at work. Based on their remarks, owners or managers of funeral homes may want to consider new hiring practices and implementing training programs for their employees.

EI and Hiring Employees

Working in the funeral industry is a service and people business. As such, a person's people skills, temperament, and personality often can be a predictor for success[95] in this profession. Research has shown us that EI is often the best indicator to look at when hiring, yet it is often overlooked during interviews in favor of hard data[96]. Hard data includes things like a person's level of education, job experience, years in the profession, etc.

I know in some markets finding any candidates is challenging, so I can understand why many owners may think it is a necessity to hire the first "normal"-looking funeral director that comes along. There is a definite cost to hiring the wrong employee, though. Think of the marketing expense of posting the position on different websites, the cost of training, and the cost of turnover if a person leaves and you have to start the hiring process all over again.

Taking your time and strategically interviewing candidates is vital. This means having structured interviews that elicit people's competencies and challenge them with some tough questions. The use of structured interviews has been proven to predict a successful hire[96]. Your interview should include specific questions on behaviors[96]. For example, don't ask, "What do you think of workplace conflict?" Instead, ask, "Tell me about a workplace conflict you were involved in and how you handled it." This gets at the heart of a person's abilities to problem-solve, manage emotions, and reach end goals. Here are some ideas you can use:

1. What causes you stress at work?
2. Can you tell me about a specific stressful encounter and how you handled it?
3. Tell me about a time when you were able to defuse a stressful situation at work.
4. How do you de-stress?

While listening to the answers to these questions, you should be analyzing the responses. Does the person seem easily stressed out? If they mention other people cause them stress, were they able to manage their reaction, and were they able to reach their desired outcome from that encounter?

Learning how someone defused a stressful situation indicates how well a person can pivot and redirect the conversation. Ultimately that shows that they can use emotions successfully.

Finally, do the potential job candidate's de-stressors seem healthy? If a person cannot give you specific de-stressors, there is a good chance the person is using unhealthy coping mechanisms.

You only get one shot to hire the best candidate. Try to find one that exhibits excellent EI skills as it will enhance a person's ability to thrive at your funeral home. Not only will the person be more successful, but hiring the best, most qualified staff improves a funeral home's odds at making the funeral a positive experience for the families you are serving.

EI Training Programs

Research also shows that employees with higher EI have better work behavior and better attitudes[97]. Better work behavior leads to better client care[98]. By offering training programs in EI, funeral directors may be better able to handle stressful situations at work, and this could then improve their retention rate.

There are many good EI training programs currently available online. I would recommend utilizing one that offers either group training sessions or on-site training options. I would also recommend that before any EI training, each person on staff that will be involved in the training should take an EI assessment. You can find several self-assessments available online, but to do a complete EI ability assessment, you will need to find a practitioner who can administer and analyze results.

Let me review the difference between the two different types of assessments available: ability-based EI tests, and trait-based EI tests. Ability-based tests stem from the belief that EI is a mental ability and includes questions that test a person's skills in perceiving, understanding, managing, and utilizing emotions to solve problems. On the other hand, trait-based EI tests view EI more as emotion and personality-related disposition, and they assess a person's EI by using a self-reporting questionnaire. Experts contend that ability-based tests are the best choice for measurement and should, therefore, be used during the hiring process to select a candidate with excellent EI skills[64]. Also, if the goal is to improve an employee's EI, ability-based EI tests should be used, as these are accurate in detecting a person's EI development[64].

Another recommendation would be to train funeral directors on how to regulate, control, and manage their emotions. Regulating emotions is a crucial component of Mayer and Salovey's EI theory[62], and that comes into play during stressful situations. EI practitioners can help identify ways to limit impulsivity and being reactionary. They can teach funeral directors how to look at a stressful situation differently, so it is viewed more as a challenge than a threat, thus helping to create more feelings of eustress rather than distress.

Finally, practitioners can also help funeral directors to learn more adaptive coping techniques. This study found that turning to religion, outside activities, peer support, and mental escapes often were very helpful with stress management for these participants. Some funeral directors will need retraining in this area as they may be accustomed to resorting to defense mechanisms like shutting down emotionally or internalizing. These maladaptive coping strategies can help momentarily but will not help manage stress in the long-term[99]. Specific EI training activities are provided in the next chapter.

Questions to Ponder

1. Do you believe these findings can extend to funeral directors outside the study group? Why or why not?

   _____

   _____

   _____

2. What do you think other funeral directors could learn from this study?

   _____

   _____

   _____

3. Have you ever been involved in an EI training program, or are you open to participating in one?

   _____

   _____

   _____

4. Based on your experiences, which one of the four EI components (perceiving, understanding, managing, or utilizing emotions) do you think needs the most attention in a training program? Why?

   _____

   _____

   _____

Tips to Improve Your EI skills

This study clearly shows that EI makes a difference for funeral directors. EI helps people communicate better and have less stress, and that, in turn, leads to better, more well-adjusted funeral directors. But even those with good EI still experience stressful moments at work. That is unavoidable to some extent. How people react and handle situations is still under their control though. You can improve your EI and therefore your ability to handle any situation that comes your way.

I subscribe to Mayer and Salovey's EI theory, which contends that there are four components to EI: perceiving emotions, understanding emotions, managing emotions, and utilizing emotions[62]. Let's look at some exercises, adapted from a teacher's EI activity workbook[100], to help improve each of these components.

Perceiving Emotions

Being able to perceive emotions in yourself and others correctly is extremely important in decision-making. If your assessment is wrong about what a person is feeling, you are off to a bad start that could negatively affect your ability to conclude this interaction successfully. Perceiving emotions in yourself requires good self-awareness. If you can recognize an emotion as it occurs, you are more likely able to deal with it. Viewing emotions in others requires proper attention to both verbal and nonverbal cues.

There are many books on the subject of body language and how to read the cues. I would suggest you read up on this subject if you feel you have difficulty perceiving emotion in other people. Here are some great contextual clues to be on the lookout for when you are interacting with other people[101].

Contextual Clue:	What it Means:
Raised eyebrows	Disbelief
Head turned away from speaker while looking down	Negative attitude
Arms open with palms extended upwards	Open and nonthreatening
Eyebrows turned down	Anger
Smile that does not reach the eyes	Fear
Arms folded across chest	Defensive
Looking down the nose at a person	Feeling superior

An important activity (see Figure 1.1) to enhance your ability to perceive emotions is one that is self-reflective and occurs after a stressful encounter. I suggest you do this towards the end of the day as that will give you more time to reflect on what happened, and that time may broaden your perspective.

Exercise 1: Enhancing Ability to Perceive Emotions

1. For starters, record what happened in the interaction

2. Then, write down what emotions you were feeling.

3. Next, write down what emotion you think the other person was feeling.

4. Finally, note what contextual clues helped you come to that decision.

As you are just learning this skill set, writing down this information helps you to process what happened in more detail. As you become more skilled, you will eventually be able to do these steps in your head, sometimes while the event is happening. The more you practice this exercise, the better you will become at spotting signals as to what the other person may be feeling. You will also get better at recognizing your own emotions. The sooner you realize these emotions, the quicker you can either regulate them or modify the situation to help reach your desired results.

While you are learning this skill, you might consider sharing your notes with a trusted colleague or friend. Do they notice the same emotion in others based on the contextual clues you provided? This sharing activity is even more beneficial if the other person witnessed the interaction. A witness' insight can help you gain a different perspective.

	EXAMPLE	Actual Scenario
Describe a stressful situation at work.	I got stressed out when I had to talk to adult children about the disposition of their mother.	
What emotion were you feeling?	Frustration and anger	
What emotion did you notice in other people?	Anger	
Describe contextual clues.	Raised voices, frowns, crossed arms	

Figure 1. Perceiving Emotion Activity

Understanding Emotions

Working in the funeral industry, how many times has one of the families yelled at you? I know it happens more frequently than you'd like. They are angry, but are they mad at you? People with low EI will say that a person is a jerk, and they will feel personally attacked. People with higher EI, though, will realize that anger may not have anything to do with you or what you just did or say. Instead, they will recognize the person may be angry because their loved one just died or because they are unprepared for this financial cost, etc.

Being reactionary is not helpful in these situations, nor is it useful in managing stress. If you can learn to understand feelings, you will be better able to handle the stressful situation by not taking it personally, and not reacting unprofessionally. Relating and understanding other's thoughts and actions is a significant way to increase one's emotional development[80].

For this exercise (see Figure 2), let's expound on the previous one by simply adding one column: possible causes for emotion.

Exercise 2: Enhancing Ability to Understanding Emotions:

1. Record what happened in the interaction.
2. Write down what emotion you were feeling.
3. Write down what emotion you think the other person was feeling.
4. Describe what contextual clues helped you come to that conclusion.
5. List possible reasons for their emotions.

In this exercise you are adding to the last activity by not only recognizing the emotions you and the other person are experiencing, but you are also thinking about why those feelings are occurring. I recommend that you do not rush through this exercise but reflect on the interaction and spend some time thinking about the "why."

If we can understand emotions better, we have a better chance of reacting appropriately in tense situations. If we misread why a person feels a certain way, we will likely respond inappropriately, causing the interaction to decline. This exercise helps with the vital regulation

	EXAMPLE	Actual Scenario
Describe stressful situation	Discussion with adult children about the disposition of their deceased mother	
What emotion/s did that trigger in you?	Frustration Irritation Anger	
Why?	I felt frustrated and angry because they were raising their voices at me.	
What emotion/s did you see in the other person?	Anger	
Describe contextual clues that helped you reach that conclusion	Raised voice Frowns Crossed arms	
Possible causes for their emotion.	They may have been angry because their mom just died or because their sibling had not been around as much.	

Figure 2. Understanding Emotions Activity

strategy of reappraisal. Thinking of possible whys for behavior enables you to stop making kneejerk decisions about what just happened.

This exercise can also help you increase your empathy and compassion. Instead of just thinking certain people are jerks, you may start to see them as individuals who may be struggling with something emotionally or physically, and they may not be handling it in the best way possible. Knowing someone is hurting can help you reframe the situation.

Managing Emotions

As I found in my study, managing emotions was the most challenging component of EI for some of my student's participants. They might have been able to perceive and understand others' emotions correctly, but they were not good at managing their own emotions. Those that could manipulate and manage their feelings were much more resilient and did not seem as negatively impacted by stress.

For starters, don't take things personally. When a person yells or cries at you, it is easy to think it is because of something that you have done. That leads you to feeling personally attacked and leads to negative emotions of your own. Try to detach yourself from the situation by keeping your emotions under control. As the old saying goes, you cannot control what happens to you, but you can control how you respond.

Here are some easy strategies that are helpful when confronted with something stressful. For starters, remind yourself not to react immediately. Whether that is counting to ten before responding or leaving the room to compose yourself, it is essential to think before you speak. Gasoline thrown on a fire intensifies the situation, and so do angry words thrown on top of angry words. Do not jump to conclusions. Check yourself the moment negative thoughts start clouding up.

For this exercise (see Figure 3), remember a time at work when someone yelled at you, and you did not handle the situation well. Write down your answers to the following questions as honestly as possible while reliving that moment.

Exercise 3: Enhancing Ability to Regulate Emotions

1. Describe the situation.
2. Describe how you reacted.
3. Analyze your effectiveness.
4. Describe other possible options.

This exercise helps you become more conscious of your actions. This will help you develop better self-awareness and become more empathetic. Think about these questions whenever you are confronted with a stressful situation. Doing this exercise will help you recognize both positive and negative emotions you are feeling and help you deal proactively with the situation.

What happened?	
How did you react in the situation?	
How effective was your strategy?	
How could you have handled the situation differently?	

Figure 3. Managing Emotions Activity

A person cannot avoid all stress all the time. We know that. The idea is not to let our stress or stressful situations get out of control. We know that work stress can affect us negatively and that prolonged exposure to stress can cause mental health problems like depression and anxiety and may eventually lead to job burnout. Adaptive coping skills are, therefore, of utmost importance. Here are some suggested ways to help you deal with stress when it occurs:

- Take a mental break by distancing yourself from the situation. Whether that is taking a walk outside, or unwinding with some television or music, this can help you relax. Even a short break gives you the needed time to be reflective, relaxed, and recharged.

- Don't dwell on a negative experience. That only gives it more importance in your mind and can cause your hippocampus to convert this short-term memory into long-term memory. Let it go!

- If you did make a mistake, admit it. All too often, we want to blame other people. If you can acknowledge you did something wrong, the stressful situation can turn into a learning opportunity. Even just asking yourself, "How could I have handled the situation differently?" can help you interpret the experience in a more positive light.

- Control your self-talk. Experts say that 95% of our emotions result from self-talk or what we say to ourselves during stressful situations[83]. Do not beat yourself up. Instead, practice using positive words.

- Do not suffer alone. People need people, so make sure you have someone in your life that you can talk to about your problems. You can turn to a coworker or family member. Again, having another person involved can help you see a different perspective. Make sure you chose this person wisely. You need someone that will not just say "you poor thing" but will instead challenge you to look at the situation differently.

- If you don't have someone you can talk to, try journaling. Not only does this give you a place to vent, but it also provides you with opportunities to go back and reflect on your thoughts and actions to assess how you could have handled the situation better.

- Laughter is great medicine. It has been shown to lower levels of cortisone and other hormones triggered by stress. Studies have shown that laughter can have positive effects on both your immune system and your mental health[102]. So, take in a comedy show, share a joke with a friend, or watch a funny movie. Anything that makes you laugh.

- To lower feelings of anxiety, practice taking deep breaths. You may benefit from meditation. There are phone apps you can download, which give you short, guided sessions to help you calm down and recharge. A simple exercise to try is to take a long, deep, inhale, and then exhale for twice as long[103]. Repeat this for a total of eight minutes and try to clear your thoughts by focusing only on your breathing. Deep breathing helps to slow your heartbeat and lower your blood pressure, and it's also a great way to lower stress[58].

Utilizing Emotions

Utilizing emotions is all about using emotions to reach a desired goal or conclusion. For funeral directors, the goal may be to have a flawless funeral or to have pleased clients that will use you again or refer others to you. Whatever that goal is, you have to be consciously aware of it.

For this exercise (see Figure 4), the goal is to be able to identify the right emotions you need to use to enhance the energy of the interaction or the direction a conversation is going. Some emotions work better in specific situations.

Exercise 4: Enhancing Ability to Utilize Emotions

1. List how at-need conferences affect you.
2. List how at-need conferences affect the bereaved.
3. List what you currently do to create your mood.
4. List what you currently do to create the mood for the bereaved.
5. List specific activities you must carry out during at-need conferences.
6. List what the desired mood would be for each activity.
7. List what you could do to create that mood.

It is essential to think about this before an actual at-need conference. By being mentally prepared and coming up with tangible goals and specific things you can do to reach that goal, you have a better likelihood of a successful meeting. Preparing is more than collecting all the necessary documents and cleaning up the conference room. I suggest that you do this exercise ahead of time and then review it afterward with a trusted colleague. Find out your colleague's techniques for reaching desired emotional states in others and try them yourself.

In addition to this exercise, mentally keep your mind fixed on the big picture. What are your top three work goals? Reflect on each of them and then think back to the

At-Need Conferences	
How does it affect me?	
How does it affect others?	
Mood at Conference	
How do I create my mood?	
How do I create others' moods?	

Specific Circumstances		
Specific Activity	Desired Mood	How do I Create that Mood?

Figure 4. Utilizing Emotions Activity Sheet

last month on the job. What obstacles did you encounter which threatened one of your goals? How did you behave in those situations? What could you have responded differently, and how could that have affected the outcome?

The use of questions such as these really opens your mind to different possibilities, options, and choices. Instead of just acting out of habit or being reactionary to a situation, you start to learn there are different ways to handle these situations. Learning that you have the ability to control your emotions and difficult situations gives you power.

It is important to remember that you will not successfully handle every situation. Sometimes things happen that you were unprepared for and so you may not respond as effectively as possible. That is okay. Every problem is a learning opportunity. Reflect on a situation and ask yourself what you learned from that experience. Every problem or stressor you face makes you stronger and better prepared for your next encounter.

This chapter has provided you with some quick and easy training recommendations. There are many more in-depth training courses available online. Increasing your EI is a work in progress. Challenge yourself to work on your EI skills over the next six months to a year and then retake the EI assessment. Since EI is an ability, the more you train in this area, the more likely you are to see improvements.

Questions to Ponder

1. How can you incorporate what you've learned about EI into your hiring practice?

_____

_____

_____

2. How do you think this chapter's exercises can be used by you or your team?

_____

_____

_____

3. What one stress management technique from this chapter can you start putting into practice?

_____

_____

_____

4. What top three work goals do you want to start focusing on?

_____

_____

_____

Epilogue

This book has been a real labor of love. I love the funeral industry. Working alongside the professionals in this industry is so rewarding. Many funeral directors feel their profession is a calling, and I could not agree more. They face so many challenges that most of us would never volunteer to take on. Funeral directors provide a real gift to the families that they serve.

I owe the funeral industry a huge thank you. First, I would like to thank all of the funeral directors that I have worked with over the past decade. I have learned so much from you and respect the work that you do. Secondly, I owe a huge thanks to those of you that participated in my study. I kept your names and any identifiers out of this book to protect your identity, but I could not have done this without you. Your contributions help further our collective knowledge about emotional intelligence and occupational stress.

I want to point out that improving EI is not a one-time event. You cannot just read this book and run through the exercises and think, "Okay, now I've got it." While studies have shown that EI training is beneficial, that training must be reinforced over time. Most funeral directors are required to obtain continuing education.

I highly recommend seeking out CE courses on EI. You can also find great tips and courses online, so start exploring and find the best option for you. You will not only be a better funeral director by improving your EI, but the effects will spill over into your personal life. Here's to working to improve ourselves and this industry that we all love!

Glossary

Ability EI – Cognitive abilities involving perceiving, understanding, managing, and utilizing emotions that can be evaluated through performance testing.

Burnout – Occurs when a person is exposed to ongoing physical and mental exhaustion on the job, which leads to emotional exhaustion, cynicism, and a decline in feeling personal accomplishment.

Compassion Fatigue – Type of secondary traumatic stress affecting those who work in caring professions that results from repeatedly being exposed to other people's grief and trauma.

Critical Incident Stress – Stress caused by exposure to tragedies, death, and life-threatening experiences. Lasts anywhere from two days to four weeks.

Depersonalization – The ability to detach oneself from feelings which results in a flat, impersonal, or callous attitude.

Dirty work – Any type of work that is deemed to be tainted, whether for social, moral, or physical reasons. A type of social stigma.

Disenfranchised grief – Occurs when a person is not able to share feelings of sadness with others, or those feelings are not recognized by others.

Display rules – Unspoken work rules that are prevalent within service industries. Require a person to conceal any emotions that are deemed negative and unacceptable.

Emotional detachment – A person's ability to detach emotionally from either a situation or a person in order to accomplish a given task. This is a coping mechanism to avoid painful emotions.

Emotive dissonance – Conflict a person feels when inner emotions do not match the feelings being expressed.

Emotional exhaustion – A main sign of burnout. Includes feeling overextended or out of emotional resources.

Emotional intelligence – A person's ability to manage and use emotions to solve problems and enhance performance.

Emotional labor – Use of emotions based on an organization's norms regardless of actual personal feelings.

Emotional regulation – The ability to control one's emotions in order to meet a desired outcome or achieve a desired goal.

General Adaptation Syndrome – Theory by Hans Selye that posits stress occurs after being exposed to a force that triggers first an alarm stage, followed by a stage of resistance, and then a stage of exhaustion.

High-stress professions – According to Karasek's job demand-control (JDC) model, high-stress professions are those that have high job demands, such as workload and time constraints. These professions require attention to detail, the ability to adjust depending on situation, and good emotional management.

Interpretative phenomenological analysis (IPA) – A type of qualitative research design that provides descriptive narratives of a person's lived experiences as well as the researcher's interpretation of events.

Occupational stress – Physical or mental stress caused by unhealthy work conditions. Occurs when employees feel they cannot handle the demands being placed on them.

Phenomenon – Term used in qualitative research to describe an experience that has been assigned meaning by a person.

Physical taint – Working in a profession that exposes workers to disgusting items such as trash or dead bodies.

Psychological distress – Condition involving both anxiety and depression caused by chronic stress.

Stigma – Negative perception someone has about another person or class of people based on social attitudes or beliefs.

Stress management – Ability to manage and process emotions in a healthy way.

Trait EI – Sees emotional intelligence as an aspect of personality.

Index

EI Exercises

Exercise 1. Perceiving Emotions

	EXAMPLE	Actual Scenario
Describe a stressful situation at work.	*I got stressed out when I had to talk to adult children about the disposition of their mother.*	
What emotion were you feeling?	*Frustration and anger*	
What emotion did you notice in other people?	*Anger*	
Describe contextual clues.	*Raised voices, frowns, crossed arms*	

Exercise 2. Understanding Emotions

	EXAMPLE	Actual Scenario
Describe a stressful situation.	*Discussion with adult children about the disposition of their deceased mother*	
What emotion(s) did that trigger in you?	*Frustration Irritation Anger*	
Why?	*I felt frustrated and angry because they were raising their voices at me.*	
What emotion(s) did you see in the other person?	*Anger*	
Describe contextual clues that helped you reach that conclusion	*Raised voice Frowns Crossed arms*	
Possible causes for their emotion.	*They may have been angry because their mom just died or because their sibling had not been around as much.*	

Exercise 3. Managing Emotions

What happened?	
How did you react in the situation?	
How effective was your strategy?	
How could you have handled the situation differently?	

Exercise 4. Utilizing Emotions

At-Need Conferences	
How does it affect me?	
How does it affect others?	
Mood at Conference	
How do I create my mood?	
How do I create others' moods?	

Specific Circumstances		
Specific Activity	Desired Mood	How do I Create that Mood?

Notes

Note: This book contains quotes, findings, and research discoveries from the following sources.

1. Sahoo, D. R., & Kharat, P. D. (2017). Emotional intelligence: Managing stress and anxiety at workplace. *International Journal of Multifaceted and Multilingual Studies*, 4(10), 88-93. Retrieved from http://ijmmsind.com/index.php/ijmms/article/view/599
2. Ford, M. T., Matthews, R. A., Wooldridge, J. D., Mishra, V., Kakar, U. M., & Strahan, S.R. (2014). How do occupational stressor-strain effects vary with time? A review and meta-analysis of the relevance of time lags in longitudinal studies. *Work & Stress*, 28(1), 9-30. doi:10.1080/02678373.2013.877096
3. Pazzanese, C. (2016, July 12). The high price of workplace stress. *Harvard Gazette*, Retrieved from https://news.harvard.edu/gazette/story/2016/07/the-high-price-of-workplace-stress/
4. Murthy, V. (2017, September). A nation under pressure: The public health consequences of stress in America [Speech]. Retrieved from https://nccih.nih.gov/news/events/lectures/SES17
5. Demerouti, E., Bakker, A. B., Nachreiner, F., & Schaufeli, W. B. (2001). The job demands-resources

model of burnout. Journal of Applied Psychology, 86, 499-512. doi:10.1037/0021-9010.86.3.499

6. van Woerkom, M., Bakker, A. B., & Nishii, L. H. (2016). Accumulative job demands and support for strength use: Fine-tuning the job demands-resources model using conservation of resources theory. *Journal of Applied Psychology, 101*(1), 141-150. Retrieved from https://digitalcommons.ilr.cornell.edu/cgi/viewcontent.cgi?article=2262&context=articles

7. Goldfarb, R., & Ben-Zur, H. (2017). Resource loss and gain following military reserve duty in Israel: An assessment of conservation of resources (COR) theory. *International Journal of Stress Management, 24*(2), 135-155. doi:10.1037/str0000036

8. Hobfoll, S. E. (2001). The influence of culture, community, and the nested-self in the stress process: Advancing conservation of resources theory. *Applied Psychology: An International Review, 50,* 337-421. doi:10.1111/1464-0597.00062

9. Selye, H. (1950). Stress and the general adaptation syndrome. *British Medical Journal, 1*(4667), 1383-1392. Retrieved from https://www.ncbi.nlm.nih.gov/pmc/articles/PMC2038162/pdf/brmedj03603-0003.pdf

10. Frankl, V. (1959). *Man's Search for Meaning.* Boston, MA: Beacon Press.

11. Shanafelt, T. D., Hasan, O., Dyrbye, L. N., Sinsky, C., Satele, D., Sloan, J., & West, C. P. (2015, December). Changes in burnout and satisfaction with work-life balance in physicians and the general US working population between 2011 and 2014. In 196 *Mayo*

Clinic Proceedings (Vol. 90, No. 12, pp. 1600-1613). Elsevier. doi:10.1016/j.mayocp.2015.08.023

12. Wang, Y., Zheng, L., Hu, T., & Zheng, Q. (2014). Stress, burnout, and job satisfaction: Case of police force in China. *Public Personnel Management, 43*(3), 325-339. doi:10.1177/0091026014535179

13. Wei, X., Wang, R., & MacDonald, E. (2015). Exploring the relations between student cynicism and student burnout. *Psychological Reports: Employment Psychology & Marketing, 117*(1), 103-115. doi:10.2466/14.11.PR0.117c14z6

14. Thomas, M., Kohli, V., & Choi, J. (2014). Correlates of job burnout among human services workers: Implications for workforce retention. *The Journal of Sociology & Social Welfare, 41*(1), 69-90. Retrieved from https://scholarworks.wmich.edu/jssw/vol41/iss4/1

15. Saijo, Y., Chiba, S., Yoshioka, E., Kawanishi, Y., Nakagi, Y., Ito, T., & ... Yoshida, T. (2013). Job stress and burnout among urban and rural hospital physicians in Japan. *Australian Journal of Rural Health, 21*(4), 225-231. doi:10.1111/ajr.12040

16. Rath, K. S., Huffman, L. B., Phillips, G. S., Carpenter, K. M., & Fowler, J. M. (2015). Burnout and associated factors among members of the Society of Gynecologic Oncology. *American Journal of Obstetrics and Gynecology, 213*(6), 824.e1-825.e9. doi:10.1016/j.ajog.2015.07.036

17. Bidlan, J. S., & Sihag, A. (2014). Occupational stress, burnout, coping and emotional intelligence: Exploring gender differences among different occupational groups of healthcare professionals. *Indian*

Journal of Health & Wellbeing, *5*(3), 299. Retrieved from http://eds.b.ebscohost.com.lopes.idm.oclc.org/eds/pdfviewer/pdfviewer?vid=2&sid=49b2a623-9cec-4151-8c66-0844d2ed8b75%40sessionmgr101

18. Sluss, D., & Powley, E. (2020). Build your team's resilience – from home. *Harvard Business Review*, Mar/Apr. Retrieved from https://hbr.org/2020/04/build-your-teams-resilence-from-home.org

19. McEwen, B. S., Bowles, N. P., Gray, J. D., Hill, M. N., Hunter, R. G., Karatsoreos, I. N., & Nasca, C. (2015). Mechanisms of stress in the brain. *Nature Neuroscience*, *18*(10), 1353-1363. doi:10.1038/nn.4086

20. Patnaik, G. (2014). Life skill enhancement strategies to minimize stress. *Social Science International*, *30*(2), 281. Retrieved from https://lopes.idm.oclc.org/login?url=http://search.ebscohost.com/login.aspx?direct=true&db=edsbl&AN=RN360544033&site=eds-live&scope=site

21. Kivimäki, M., Jokela, M., Nyberg, S. T., Singh-Manoux, A., Fransson, E. I., Alfredsson, L., . . . Virtanen, M. (2015). Long working hours and risk of coronary heart disease and stroke: A systematic review and meta-analysis of published and unpublished data for 603 838 individuals. *The Lancet*, *386*(10005), 1739-1746. doi:10.1016/S0140-6736(15)60295-1

22. Blanc-Lapierre, A., Rousseau, M., Weiss, D., El-Zein, M., Siemiatycki, J., & Parent, M. (2017). Lifetime report of perceived stress at work and cancer among men: A case-control study in Montreal, Canada. *Preventive Medicine*, *96*, 28-35. doi:10.1016/j.ypmed.2016.12.004

23. Makhija, P., Naidu, G., & TN, R. (2017). A comparative study of ORS among the age group of women's working in selective services. *Pacific Business Review International*, 9(12), 113-122. Retrieved from http://www.pbr.co.in/2017/June.aspx

24. Devonish, D., Kouvonen, A., & Coyne, I. (2012). The justice-workplace health relationship: The mediating role of emotions. *International Journal of Workplace Health Management*, 5(2), 88-103. doi:10.1108/17538351211239144

25. Demerouti, E., Bakker, A. B., & Leiter, M. (2014). Burnout and job performance: The moderating role of selection, optimization, and compensation strategies. *Journal of Occupational Health Psychology*, 19(1), 96. doi:10.1037/a0035062

26. Quinones, C., Rodriguez-Carvajal, R., & Griffiths, M. D. (2017). Testing a eustress-distress emotion regulation model in British and Spanish front-line employees. *International Journal of Stress Management*, 241-28. Retrieved from http://irep.ntu.ac.uk/id/eprint/28002/1/PubSub5529_Griffiths.pdf

27. Kozusznik, M. W., Rodríguez, I., & Peiró, J. M. (2015). Eustress and distress climates in teams: Patterns and outcomes. *International Journal of Stress Management*, 22(1), 1-23. doi:10.1037/a0038581

28. Chiva, R., & Habib, J. (2015). A framework for organizational learning: Zero, adaptive and generative learning. *Journal of Management and Organization*, 21(3), 350-368. doi:10.1017/jmo.2014.88

29. Ludlum, K. G., Ludlum, M., & Alsobrook, L. (2014). Job satisfaction and media image for workers in the

Texas funeral industry: A preliminary investigation. *Business Journal for Entrepreneurs, 2, 29-37.*

30. Hyland, L., & Morse, J. (1995). Orchestrating comfort: The role of funeral directors. *Death Studies, 19,* 453-474.

31. Hughes, E. C. (1951). Work and the self. In J.H. Rohrer & M. Sherif (Eds.), Social psychology at the crossroads. New York: Harper & Brothers.

32. Petri, A.E. (2020, April 16). Someone has died. That's when their job begins. *The New York Times.* Retrieved from https://www.nytimes.com/2020/04/16/opinion/coronavirus-funeral-directors.amp.html?smid=em-share

33. Anderson, T. (2020, April 22). What about "Demand"? Funeral Director Daily. Retrieved from www.funeraldirectordaily.com/what-about-demand/

34. Rivenburg, R. (1992, August 21). The last laugh: Those in funeral industry cope with gloom, grief using their own brand of humor. *Los Angeles Times.* Retrieved from http://articles.latimes.com/1992-08-21/news/vw-5583_1_funeral-industry

35. Wilde, C. (2017, January 10). Confessions of a funeral director. [Facebook post]. Retrieved from https://m.facebook.com/story.php?story_fbid=1843828102308209&id=192751080749261

36. Kroshus, J., & Swarthout, D. (1995). Critical incident stress among funeral directors: Identifying factors relevant for mental health. *Journal of Mental Health Counseling, 17*(4), 441. Retrieved from https://lopes.idm.oclc.org/login?url=http://search.ebscohost.com/login.aspx?direct=true&db=ehh&AN=9702241002&site=eds-live&scope=site

37. Mayer, D. M. (2018). Critical Incidents in Health Care. *MEDSURG Nursing*, 27(4), 231–237. Retrieved from https://lopes.idm.oclc.org/login?url=http://search.ebscohost.com/login.aspx?direct=true&db=ccm&AN=131366463&site=eds-live&scope=site Mastracci & Hsieh, 2016

38. Gutierrez, D., & Mullen, P. R. (2016). Emotional intelligence and the counselor: Examining the relationship of trait emotional intelligence to counselor burnout. *Journal of Mental Health Counseling*, 38(3), 187-200. doi:10.1174/mehc.38.3.01

39. Truszczyńska, A., Scherer, A., & Drzał-Grabiec, J. (2016). The occurrence of overload at work and musculoskeletal pain in young physiotherapists. *Work*, 54(3), 609-616. doi:10.3233/WOR-162343

40. Flynn, B., McCarroll, J., & Biggs, Q. (2015). Stress and resilience in military mortuary workers: Care of the dead from battlefield to home. *Death Studies*, 39(2), 92-98. doi:10.1080/07481187.2014.893463

41. Rudd, R. A., & D'Andrea, L. M. (2015). Compassionate detachment: Managing professional stress while providing quality care to bereaved parents. *Journal of Workplace Behavioral Health*, 30,3, 287-305. doi: 10.1080/15555240.2014.999079

42. Heponiemi, T., Presseau, J., & Elovainio, M. (2016). On-call work and physicians' turnover intention: The moderating effect of job strain. Psychology, Health & Medicine, 21(1), 74-80. doi:10.1080/13548 506.2015.1051061

43. Roberts, A. L., Johnson, N. J., Cudkowicz, M. E., Eum, K., & Weisskopf, M. G. (2016). Job-related formaldehyde exposure and ALS mortality in

the USA. *Journal of Neurology, Neurosurgery and Psychiatry, 87*(7), 786. doi:10.1136/jnnp-2015-310750

44. Ladeira, C., Padua, M., Veiga, L., Viegas, S., Carolino, E., Gomes, M. C., & Brito, M. (2015). Influence of serum levels of vitamins A, D, and E as well as vitamin D receptor polymorphisms on micronucleus frequencies and other biomarkers of genotoxicity in workers exposed to formaldehyde. *Journal of Nutrigenetics and Nutrigenomics, 84*(4-6), 205-214. doi:10.1159/000444486

45. Schwartz, M. L., Jolson, M. A., & Lee, R. H. (1986). The marketing of funeral services: Past, present, and future. *Business Horizons, 29*(2), 40. doi:10.1016/0007-6813(86)90068-6

46. Wu, H., Liu, L., Wang, Y., Gao, F., Zhao, X., & Wang, L. (2013). Factors associated with burnout among Chinese hospital doctors: A cross-sectional study. *BMC Public Health, 13*(1), 786. doi:10.1186/1471-2458-13-786

47. Kochanek, K., Murphy, S., Xu, J., & Tejada-Vera, B. (2016). Deaths: Final data for 2014. *National Vital Statistics Reports, 65*(4). Retrieved from: https://www.cdc.gov/nchs/data/nvsr/nvsr65/nvsr65_04.pdf

48. van Mol, M. M. C., Kompanje, E. J. O., Benoit, D. D., Bakker, J., & Nijkamp, M. D. (2015). The Prevalence of Compassion Fatigue and Burnout among Healthcare Professionals in Intensive Care Units: A Systematic Review. *PLoS ONE, 10*(8), e0136955.

49. Rivers, M., & Haycock, E. (2015). Natural or unnerving. *Australian Parks & Leisure, 18*(3), 22-24. Retrieved from https://search.informit.com.au/documentSummary;dn=875846943941761;res=IELHSS

50. Thompson, W. E. (1991). Handling the stigma of handling the dead: Morticians and funeral directors. *Deviant Behavior, 12*(4), 403-429. Retrieved from http://neoliberalfeminism.com/wp-content/uploads/2018/03/The-Time-Bind.pdf#page=83

51. Mastracci, S., & Hsieh, C. (2016). Emotional labor and job stress in caring professions: Exploring universalism and particularism in construct and culture. *International Journal of Public Administration, 39*(14), 1125-1133. doi:10.1080/01900692.2015.1068327

52. Smith, J. R., Dorsey, K. D., & Mosley, A. L. (2009). Licensed funeral directors: An empirical analysis of the dimensions and consequences of emotional labor. *International Management Review, 5*(2), 30-43. Retrieved from https://lopes.idm.oclc.org/login?url=http://search.ebscohost.com/login.aspx?direct=true&db=bth&AN=45344641&site=eds-live&scope=site

53. Yagil, D. (2015). Display rules for kindness: Outcomes of suppressing benevolent emotions. *Motivation and Emotion, 39*(1), 156-166. doi:10.1007/s11031-014-9418-1

54. LeDoux, J. (1998). Fear and the brain: Where have we been, and where are we going? Biological Psychiatry, 44, 1229–1238. Retrieved from https://www.psychiatry.wisc.edu/courses/Nitschke/seminar/ledoux_1998_bio_psych.pdf

55. Immordino-Yang, M. H., & Singh, V. (2013). Hippocampal contributions to the processing of social emotions. *Human brain mapping, 34*(4), 945-955. Retrieved from https://onlinelibrary.wiley.com/doi/pdf/10.1002/hbm.21485

56. Ghashghaei, H. T., Hilgetag, C. C., & Barbas, H. (2007). Sequence of information processing for emotions based on the anatomic dialogue between prefrontal cortex and amygdala. *NeuroImage*, *34*(3), 905–923. doi:10.1016/j.neuroimage.2006.09.046

57. Barbas, H. (1995). Anatomic basis of cognitive-emotional interactions in the primate prefrontal cortex. *Neuroscience and Biobehavioral Reviews*, *19*(3), 499-510. doi:0149-7634(94)00053-0

58. Cunningham, S. (2018, September 19). Understanding breathing and the importance of taking a deep breath. *UCHealth Today*. Retrieved from www.uchealth.org/today/understanding-breathing-and-the-importance-of-taking-a-deep-breath/

59. Gondal, U.H., & Husain, T. (2012). A comparative study of intelligence quotient and emotional intelligence: Effect on employees' performance. *Asian Journal of Business Management*, *5*(1), 153-162. Retrieved from https://pdfs.semanticscholar.org/72b3/789ace98a9a172110586e305accc4b0a2652.pdf

60. Braaten, E.B., & Norman, D. (2006). Intelligence (IQ) Testing. *Pediatrics in Review*, *27*(11), 403-408. Retrieved from https://www.researchgate.net/profile/Ellen_Braaten/publication/6716188_Intelligence_IQ_Testing/links/02e7e53b44aafd26b5000000/Intelligence-IQ-Testing.pdf

61. McPhail, K. (2004). An emotional response to the state of accounting education: Developing accounting students' emotional intelligence. Critical Perspectives on Accounting, 15, 629–648. doi:10.1016/S1045-2354(03)0050-9

62. Mayer, J. D., & Salovey, P. (1993). The intelligence of emotional intelligence. Intelligence, 17, 433-442. Retrieved from https://eclass.teicrete.gr/modules/document/file.php/IP-ERLSF116/Mayer-Salovey.1993-libre.pdf

63. Gohm, C. L., Corser, G. C., & Dalsky, D. J. (2005). Emotional intelligence under stress: Useful, unnecessary, or irrelevant? *Personality and Individual Differences*, *39*(6), 1017-1028. doi:10.1016/j.paid.2005.03.018

64. Asthana, A., & Lodhwal, R. K. (2017). Concepts and measures of emotional intelligence: A conceptual study. *International Journal of Engineering Technology Science and Research*, *4*(8), 1243-1250. Retrieved from http://www.ijetsr.com/images/short_pdf/1503914898_1243-1250-mccia876-ijetsr.pdf

65. Frajo-Apor, B., Pardeller, S., Kemmler, G., & Hofer, A. (2016) Emotional Intelligence and resilience in mental health professionals caring for patients with serious mental illness, *Psychology, Health & Medicine*, *21*(6), 755-761, doi 10.1080/13548506.2015.1120325

66. Mayer, J. D., Salovey, P., & Caruso, D. R. (2004). Emotional intelligence: Theory, findings, and implications. *Psychological Inquiry*, *15*(3), 197-215. Retrieved from https://lopes.idm.oclc.org/login?url=http://search.ebscohost.com/login.aspx?direct=true&db=bth&AN=14595133&site=eds-live&scope=site

67. Peña-Sarrionandia, A., Mikolajczak, M., & Gross, J. J. (2015). Integrating emotion regulation and emotional intelligence traditions: a meta-analysis. Frontiers in Psychology, 6. doi:10.3389/fpsyg.2015.00160

68. Dhani, P., & Sharma, T. (2017). The impact of an individual's emotional intelligence on his/her job

performance: An empirical study in Indian context. *International Business Management*, 11(7), 1419-1428. Retrieved from http://docsdrive.com/pdfs/medwelljournals/ibm/2017/1419-1428.pdf

69. Schutte, N. S., & Loi, N. M. (2014). Connections between emotional intelligence and workplace flourishing. *Personality and Individual Differences, 66*, 134-139. doi:10.1016/j.paid.2014.03.031

70. Di Fabio, A., & Saklofske, D. H. (2014). Promoting individual resources: The challenge of trait emotional intelligence. *Personality and Individual Differences,* 6519-23. doi:10.1016/j.paid.2014.01.026

71. Cherniss, C., & Goleman, D. (2001). The emotionally intelligence workplace. *How to select for, measure, and improve emotional intelligence in individuals, groups and organizations.* San Francisco: Jossey-Bass.

72. Mikolajczak, M., Menil, C., & Luminet, O. (2007). Explaining the protective effect of trait emotional intelligence regarding occupational stress: Exploration of emotional labour processes. *Journal of Research in Personality, 41*(5), 1107. doi:10.1016/j.jrp.2007.001.003

73. Laborde, S., Lautenbach, F., Allen, M. S., Herbert, C., & Achtzehn, S. (2014). The role of trait emotional intelligence in emotion regulation and performance under pressure. *Personality and Individual differences, 57*, 43-47. doi:10.1016/j.paid.2013.09.013

74. Ruiz-Aranda, D., Extremera, N., & Pineda-Galán, C. (2014). Emotional intelligence, life satisfaction and subjective happiness in female student health professionals: the mediating effect of perceived stress.

Journal of psychiatric and mental health nursing, 21(2), 106-113. doi:10.1111/jpm.12052

75. Mikolajczak, M., & Luminet, O. (2008). Trait emotional intelligence and the cognitive appraisal of stressful events: An exploratory study. *Personality and individual differences, 44*(7), 1445-1453. doi:10.1016/j. paid.2007.12.012

76. Arora, S., Russ, S., Petrides, K. V., Sirimanna, P., Aggarwal, R., Darzi, A., & Sevdalis, N. (2011). Emotional intelligence and stress in medical students performing surgical tasks. *Academic Medicine, 86*(10), 1311-1317. doi:10.1097/ACM.0b013e31822bd7aa

77. Petrides, K. V., & Furnham, A. (2003). Trait emotional intelligence: Behavioural validation in two studies of emotion recognition and reactivity to mood induction. *European journal of personality, 17*(1), 39-57. doi:10.1002/per.466

78. Cheung, S. Y., Gong, Y., & Huang, J. C. (2016). Emotional intelligence, job insecurity, and psychological strain among real estate agents: A test of mediation and moderation models. *The International Journal of Human Resource Management, 27*(22), 2673-2694. doi:10.1080/09585192.2015.1091369

79. Levitt, H. M., Motulsky, S. L., Wertz, F. J., Morrow, S. L., & Ponterotto, J. G. (2017). Recommendations for designing and reviewing qualitative research in psychology: Promoting methodological integrity. *Qualitative Psychology, 4*(1), 2-22. doi:10.1037/qup0000082

80. Pietkiewicz, I., & Smith, J. A. (2014). A practical guide to using interpretative phenomenological analysis in

qualitative research psychology. *Psychological Journal*, *20*(1), 7-14. doi:10.14691/CPPJ.20.1.7

81. Gill, M. J. (2014). The possibilities of phenomenology for organizational research. *Organizational Research Methods*, *17*(2), 118-137. doi:10.1177/1094428113518348

82. Etikan, I., Musa, S. A., & Alkassim, R. S. (2016). Comparison of convenience sampling and purposive sampling. *American Journal of Theoretical and Applied Statistics*, *5*(1), 1-4. doi:10.11648/j.ajtas.20160501.11

83. Tracy, B. (2003). *Change your Thinking Change your Life*. New York, NY: MJF Books.

84. Elmore, L. C., Jeffe, D. B., Jin, L., Awad, M. M., & Turnbull, I. R. (2016). National survey of burnout among US general surgery residents. *Journal of the American College of Surgeons*, *223*(3), 440-451. doi:10.1016/j.jamcollsurg.2016.05.014

85. Nolen-Hoeksema, S., & Jackson, B. (2001). Mediators of the gender difference in rumination. *Psychology of Women Quarterly*, *25*, 37-47. doi:10.1111/1471-6402.00005

86. Hamid Rao, A. (Guest). (2020, April 13). *"We're Beyond Stretched"* [Audio Podcast]. Retrieved from http://hbr.org.

87. Liddon, L., Kingerlee, R., & Barry, J. A. (2018). Gender differences in preferences for psychological treatment, coping strategies, and triggers to help-seeking. *British Journal of Clinical Psychology*, *57*, 442-58. doi:10.1111/bjc.12147

88. Oliffe, J. L., Kelly, M. T., Bottorff, J. L., Johnson, J. L., & Wong, S. T. (2017). "He's More Typically Female Because He's Not Afraid to Cry": Connecting Heterosexual Gender Relations and Men's Depression*.

In *The Psychology of Gender and Health* (pp. 177-197). doi:10.1016/j.socscimed.2011.06.034

89. Extremera, N., Fernandez-Berrocal, P., & Salovey, P. (2006). Spanish version of the Mayer-Salovey-Caruso Emotional Intelligence Test (MSCEIT) version 2.0: Reliabilities, age, and gender differences. *Psicothema*, 18, 42-48. Retrieved from www.redalyc.org/pdf/727/72709506.pdf

90. Mayer, J. D., Caruso, D. R., & Salovey, P. (1999). Emotional intelligence meets traditional standards for an intelligence. *Intelligence*, 27, 267-298. Retrieved from www.gruberpeplab.com/teaching/psych131_fall2013/documents/13.1_Mayer_2000_EmotionalIntelligence MeetsStandsForTraditionalIntelligence.pdf

91. Santana, M. R. M., Zatti, C., Spader, M. L., Malgarim, B. G., Salle, E., Piltcher, R., ... & Freitas, L. H. (2017). Acute stress disorder and defense mechanisms: a study of physical trauma patients admitted to an emergency hospital. *Trends in psychiatry and psychotherapy*, 39(4), 247-256. doi:10.1590/2237-6089-2016-0071

92. Van Beveren, M. L., Harding, K., Beyers, W., & Braet, C. (2018). Don't worry, be happy: The role of positive emotionality and adaptive emotion regulation strategies for youth depressive symptoms. *British Journal of Clinical Psychology*, 57(1), 18-41. doi:10.1111/bjc.12151

93. Spataro, B. M., Tilstra, S. A., Rubio, D. M., & McNeil, M. A. (2016). The toxicity of self-blame: Sex differences in burnout and coping in internal medicine trainees. *Journal of Women's Health*, 25(11), 1147-1152. doi:10.1089/jwh.2015.5604

94. Roos, L. G., Levens, S. M., & Bennett, J. M. (2018). Stressful life events, relationship stressors, and cortisol reactivity: The moderating role of suppression. *Psychoneuroendocrinology*, 89, 69-77. doi:10.1016/j.psyneuen.2017.12.026

95. Richard, L. (1999). Hiring emotionally intelligent associates. *Law Prac. Q.*, *1,7*.

96. Fernandez-Araoz, C. (1999). Hiring without firing. *Harvard Business Review*, 77, 108-121. Retrieved from www.s3.amazonaws.com

97. Ugwu, L. I., Enwereuzor, I. K., Fimber, U. S., & Ugwu, D. I. (2017). Nurses' burnout and counterproductive work behavior in a Nigerian sample: The moderating role of emotional intelligence. *International Journal of Africa Nursing Sciences*, 7, 106-113. doi:10.1016/j.ijans.2017.11.004

98. Kaur, D., Sambasivan, M., & Kumar, N. (2013). Effect of spiritual intelligence, emotional intelligence, psychological ownership and burnout on caring behavior of nurses: A cross-sectional study. *Journal of Clinical Nursing*, 22, 3192-3202. doi:10.1111/jocn.12386

99. Holton, M. K., Berry, A. E., & Chaney, J. D. (2016). Employee stress management: An examination of adaptive and maladaptive coping strategies on employee health. *Work*, *53*, 299-305. doi:10.3233/WOR-152145

100. Brackett, M. A., & Katulak, N. A. (2006). Emotional intelligence in the classroom: Skill-based training for teachers and students. In J. Ciarrochi & J. D. Mayer (Eds.) *Applying Emotional Intelligence: A Practitioner's Guide*. New York, NY: Psychology Press

101. Pease, A., & Pease, B. (2004). *The Definitive Book of Body Language*. New York, NY: Bantam Dell.

102. Agarwal, S.K. (2014). Therapeutic benefits of laughter. *Medical Science*, 12(46), 19-23. Retrieved from www.discoveryjournals.org/medicalscience/current_issue/v12-13/n45-53/A4.pdf

103. Gervais, M. (2020). How to manage your stress when the sky is falling. *Harvard Business Review*, Mar/Apr. Retrieved from https://hbr.org/2020/04/how-to-manage-your-stress-when-the-sky-is-falling.org